Praise for Travis LeFever, Amanda LeFever, and *Game Changers*

Travis and Amanda expose the critical gaps between facility-centric strategy and community health reality—then show you exactly how to close them. Your status quo will be challenged. As they put it: "This book serves those who serve others."

–Nido Qubein, PhD

President, High Point University

Travis and Amanda bring a builder's practicality, a leader's vision, and a relentless focus on what actually works to a proven strategy for sustainable community health. The result: mission and margin in perfect balance.

–Paul McGann, MD

Former Deputy Chief Medical Officer, Centers for Medicare & Medicaid Services

Travis and Amanda offer an essential guide to care without walls—one written from the heart. You'll see your patients in these pages. This book is required reading for mobile opioid treatment program providers.

–Eric Morse, MD

Addiction and Sports Psychiatrist, Morse Clinics

Travis and Amanda reframe employer health strategy in a way that finally makes sense. *Game Changers* answers the questions benefits leaders are asking: Why don't employees use the coverage we provide? How do we reduce costs while improving outcomes? Read this book.

–Eric Beck

Senior Vice President, National Non-Profit Practice Leader, Marsh McLennan Agency

Travis and Amanda bring implementation experience, policy fluency, and a relentless focus on outcomes to a proven framework for community health transformation. The result: a blueprint for scaling effective health programs across the country.

–Mandy K. Cohen, MD, MPH

National Advisor, Manatt Health; former Director, Centers for Disease Control and Prevention (2023-2025); former Secretary, North Carolina Department of Health and Human Services (2017-2021); former Chief Operating Officer, Centers for Medicare and Medicaid Services (2013-2017)

As a former community health system CEO, I wish I'd had this book years ago. Travis and Amanda bring value creation from economically invisible populations to life in ways that make previous attempts feel academic by comparison. Keep it on your desk as you navigate network adequacy, community health access, and join the new momentum in building mobile healthcare infrastructure.

–David B. Vliet

VlietHealth/Mobile Health Strategies: Guatemala; former CEO, LifeLong Medical Care; founding member, Advocates for Community Health

This powerful, deeply personal journey—from losing a father to a preventable heart attack to confronting what it means to truly serve others—anchors a mission to improve healthcare delivery in our country. By turning grief into a blueprint for service, this book shows how mobile healthcare can reshape access, improve trust, and deliver quality healthcare to communities everywhere.

–Mary Kathryn Fallon

Acting Director, The Family Van and Mobile Health Map, Harvard Medical School

Travis and Amanda LeFever embody commitment to mission, determination, and an abiding belief in the inherent goodness of others. Travis frequently says, "I want more for you than I want from you," ... and he means it. The pages of this book tell the story of an extraordinary mission-driven organization with a transparent, vibrant, people-centered culture. As a lifelong student of leadership behavior, I have tremendous respect for the healthcare leaders profiled in this book. Read *Game Changers* to learn more about how patients, providers, healthcare executives, and payers are benefiting immensely from the hard work, innovation, products, and services of the exceptional team at Mission Mobile Medical.

–Dennis Wagner

Principal and Managing Director, Yes And Leadership, LLC; former senior executive, Centers for Medicare & Medicaid Services

As a physician who began practicing medicine in a patient-centered medical system in post-Soviet Ukraine, I enthusiastically endorse this important manuscript that reimagines and maps out necessary efficiencies and practicalities to be implemented in a future patient-centered healthcare system, which are unaccounted for within the current hospital-centered medical system in the USA.

–Andrew (Andriy) Batchinsky, MD

Founding Program Director and Senior Scientist, Autonomous Reanimation and Evacuation Research Institute and the Basil A. Pruitt, Jr. Innovation Center, The Geneva Foundation; Professor, Director of the Department of Translational Medicine, University of the Incarnate Word School of Osteopathic Medicine, San Antonio, Texas; Professor of Surgery and Medicine, Uniformed Services University, Bethesda, Maryland

Two of the greatest people I know, always leading with heart and passion.

–Command Sergeant Major Gretchen Evans, US Army (Retired)

Bronze Star and Purple Heart recipient; 2022 Pat Tillman Award for Service; US Army Women's Hall of Fame; Founder of Team UNBROKEN

Travis and Amanda have brought new energy and perspective to how healthcare decision-makers can more effectively improve access to healthcare for our most vulnerable neighbors. *Game Changers* answers the question executives with heart are always asking: How do we better serve our community and those patients who might never walk through our doors?

–Daniella Jaimes-Colina, PhD, MBA, MPH

Chief Executive Officer, Piedmont Health Services, Inc., North Carolina's first Federally Qualified Health Center

Through trial and error and by working with those at the front lines, at the administrative level, and at the policy level, Travis and Amanda have the direct experience in building systems that will WORK in improving the lives of those who are often not heard, and who may not even know what they need themselves. It's a significant shift in how we currently think about healthcare delivery (and, more broadly, about improving lives and communities in general), but they provide the evidence and arguments to support it.

–H. Roger Tang, PhD

Chief Technical Officer, Triple Ring Technologies

Travis and Amanda bring operational credibility, financial rigor, and a relentless focus on outcomes in their goal to bring more healthcare access to communities in need. They are steadfast in their commitment to identify and manage chronic disease early and can go where others simply cannot.

–Gordon L. Chen, MD

Chief Executive Officer, ThriveWell; ChenMed Board Member, Principal, and former Chief Medical Officer

Practical. Proven. Sustainable. Travis and Amanda deliver community health that works … on mission and on margin.

–Rich Armstrong

Former President, Great Game of Business; Executive, SRC Holdings Corporation; Board Member, National Center for Employee Ownership

Game Changers

Travis and Amanda LeFever

with Don Yaeger and Jason Cole

Game Changers

Voices from the **Front Lines of Mobile Health**

Advantage | Books

Published by Advantage Books, Charleston, South Carolina.
An imprint of Advantage Media.

ADVANTAGE is a registered trademark, and the Advantage colophon is a trademark of Advantage Media Group, Inc.

Printed in the United States of America.

10 9 8 7 6 5 4 3 2 1

ISBN: 979-8-89188-621-6 (Paperback)
ISBN: 979-8-89188-622-3 (eBook)

Library of Congress Control Number: 2026905822

Cover design by Matthew Morse.
Layout design by Ruthie Wood.

Advantage Books is an imprint of Advantage Media Group. Advantage Media helps busy entrepreneurs, CEOs, and leaders write and publish a book to grow their business and become the authority in their field. Advantage authors comprise an exclusive community of industry professionals, idea-makers, and thought leaders. For more information go to **advantagemedia.com**.

03-27-2026 3:12

To Dad—You taught me that taking care of people matters more than making money. You died before you were finished raising me, and I miss you every day. I wish you were here to see how the values, work ethic, and unconditional love that you poured into us is changing the world.

To Mom—From church to the children's home, this work puts legs to your legacy. We're doing what you taught us by your example, caring for community and helping others see the way, every day.

To Amanda—You're the steady one, the planner, the one who loves me enough to take my wild ideas and rough starts and patiently turn them into real systems that add value to people. Without you, none of this works. I love you.

To our kids, Will, Gracie, and London—You are champions. You will never understand how much you mean to all of us. We hope our lives light a path forward for each of you to go change the world in your own way. We love you.

To Justin Schultz—You're the one who made it happen. You'll never understand how grateful we are to you for your intellect, your trust, your efforts, and your heart. We love you and your family.

Contents

Foreword

By John C. Maxwell

I've been teaching leadership for more than fifty years, and one of the truths I keep coming back to is this: the people who grow the most are the ones who never stop learning. Not the convenient kind of learning, where you pick up a book now and then or attend a conference when it fits the schedule. The *hard* kind. The kind that requires you to step out of your comfort zone, go somewhere unfamiliar, and stay long enough to grow roots. That kind of learning is rare. Which is why, when I meet people who live it, I take notice.

Travis and Amanda LeFever are two of those people. I've known them for over a decade, and in that time, I've watched them do something that most people only talk about: they keep showing up. Year after year, they've leaned into growth. They've asked the hard questions, taken the notes, and *applied* what they learned to real problems, real people, real communities. And in doing so, they've begun to make a genuine difference in the lives of others.

Here's what I've noticed about Travis and Amanda: they practice three things that separate good leaders from great ones. First, they *value people*, not just the people who can help them, but *all* people. Second, they *add value to people*; they model what servant leadership looks like from the inside out. And third, they *multiply leaders*. They don't just want followers; they want to develop other leaders. That's not just a strategy. That's the heartbeat of leadership that lasts.

Those three commitments, valuing people, adding value to people, and multiplying leaders, are the foundation of this book. *Game Changers* is for the leader who wants more than a title or a platform. It's for the leader who wants to *matter*; to build something that outlasts them, to grow influence that doesn't depend on position, and to lift others as they rise. That's the kind of leadership that changes families, organizations, and communities. That's the kind of leaders Travis and Amanda are, and the kind they want to help you become.

Here's my question for you: Will you take what Travis and Amanda have written and put it to work in your leadership? Because the world doesn't need more people who know the right things. It needs more people who *do* them. I believe this book will help you become one of those people.

Your friend,
John C. Maxwell

A Note from Travis

My father once drove forty-five minutes to give money to a man he had never met.

I heard this story the night my father died, as my mother sat quietly next to me on their couch, hands in her lap, telling me stories about him. Some made us laugh, and some made us cry. This one happened on a summer Sunday at church, and it struck a chord deep inside me.

Just so you get the full picture, my family is from a little north of Wilkesboro, North Carolina, a town of about four thousand people at the base of the Blue Ridge mountain range, which is part of the larger Appalachian Mountains.

It's a beautiful part of the country that sits near the border of North Carolina and Tennessee. Everywhere you look is like the background of a Winslow Homer painting. North Wilkesboro is as rural and country as it gets, right down to the racetrack that has sat on the edge of town since 1947. Wilkes County is one of the places where stock car racing (NASCAR, as it's known more formally) got its start. I grew up a few miles from where Benny Parsons and Junior Johnson were born and raised, and where they ran moonshine through the mountains in hot-rod Fords.

Our little church sat in a clearing on the top of White Oak Mountain, and the only way up was a many-miles-long dirt-and-gravel road. On the Sunday this story took place, the congregation was in a service when one of the deacons heard the church phone ring in the back hallway. The man calling was stuck at a Walmart about forty-five minutes away and said he was out of work, out of money, out of gas, and calling for help. He just needed gas to get home to his family in Tennessee.

The circumstances were a little odd, but the man seemed desperate. The congregation talked it over and decided, for whatever reason, that helping him wasn't something they felt right about. So, when the service ended, everyone just said their amens and stood up for the usual rounds of post-sermon handshakes and hugs before heading out to lunch.

This time, however, rather than catch up with friends, my mother told me that my father took her by the hand, and they headed straight for the car. When my mom asked where they were going, my dad replied, "We're going to find that man who needs gas money." They then drove forty-five minutes down the mountain, into town, to the Walmart, and found him still at the pay phone, still calling churches.

My father gave him some money—enough for dinner, enough for gas. My father wasn't a rich man by any stretch, but he was a hardworking man. He spent most of his life as a barber, cutting hair for nearly thirty years until his hands gave out on him and he had to give it up.

But deep pockets weren't the point. My father wanted to help, and he did. The man asked for his address and about paying the money back. Instead, my dad told him to pay it forward, to help someone else someday down the line.

My father's inherent goodness had a powerful effect on everyone. He was, in so many ways, a part of everyone's life. In particular, he taught me everything I needed to know about how I should treat people.

In my father's world, valuing people was defined by actions, not by transactions. My father was a servant leader, and though I've met hundreds of servant leaders in the years since he passed, and love them all, my father remains my favorite. His kindness impacted my life in a profound way.

Introduction

In the United States, we spend significant amounts on healthcare for generally poor results, which is the very definition of a low-value health system. We've built a system that fails the people who struggle to access the care they need. The phrase *barriers to access* in healthcare is often repeated but seems backward to me, as if somehow patients are responsible for the failure of the healthcare industry to adequately distribute services. I believe that we're spending money in the wrong places.

Think about the concepts of cause and effect, reaping and sowing, investment and return. As a country, we've neglected primary care for decades, and now we're paying the price. We're reaping what we sowed. At the root of this is the role that money plays as a motivator in our society. You see this in audit studies measuring actual appointment access, in which 80 percent of calls from privately insured patients successfully scheduled appointments compared to only 45 percent of calls from Medicaid patients.[1] From the outside looking in, it can feel like if you can't pay, then people won't care.

1 Walter R. Hsiang et al., "Medicaid Patients Have Greater Difficulty Scheduling Health Care Appointments Compared with Private Insurance Patients: A Meta-Analysis," *INQUIRY: The Journal of Health Care Organization, Provision, and Financing* 56 (2019), https://doi.org/10.1177/0046958019838118.

The numbers also tell the story of people like my father, my servant leader hero, as you learned in "A Note from Travis." He was one of the sixty-six million people (one in five Americans) who live in rural areas. Those are the Americans most likely to smoke, struggle with obesity, and battle chronic conditions such as heart disease, hypertension, and diabetes. They're also more likely to die from those conditions.

Want to know how broken our system is? Nearly every American lives within ten minutes of a fire station, but rural Americans travel an average of thirty-four minutes to reach a doctor's office—nine minutes longer than their urban counterparts.[2] And it's getting worse, with 195 rural hospitals having closed since 2005[3] and another 700 at risk of closing.[4]

Fighting the Good Fight

Working to right this wrong is the better tomorrow we're fighting for, and there's no doubt it's a tough fight. But what I've learned is that when fighting for something this important, you should never climb alone. And we have found many fellow travelers on this road, some of whom you'll meet in this book.

The journey for Amanda and me started out as a chance to make a steady living but has transformed into a chance to make a significant

---

2 Marvellous A. Akinlotan et al., "Travel for Medical or Dental Care by Race/Ethnicity and Rurality in the U.S.: Findings from the 2001, 2009 and 2017 National Household Travel Surveys," *Preventive Medicine Reports* 35 (2023), https://doi.org/10.1016/j.pmedr.2023.102297.

3 "195 Rural Hospital Closures and Conversions Since January 2005," NC Rural Health Research Program, The Cecil G. Sheps Center for Health Services Research, University of North Carolina at Chapel Hill, accessed December 25, 2025, www.shepscenter.unc.edu/programs-projects/rural-health/rural-hospital-closures/.

4 "The Rural Health Safety Net Under Pressure: Rural Hospital Vulnerability," Chartis Center for Rural Health, 2020, www.chartis.com/insights/rural-health-safety-net-under-pressure-rural-hospital-vulnerability.

difference in the lives of millions of Americans. For the past five years, we have spent nearly every waking hour trying to understand how, exactly, healthcare services are—and are not—delivered to people who happen to live in rural America.

We've looked high—into policy, legislation, and executive-level decision-making—and got down in the real-world weeds, going out with street medicine providers and doing patient–provider experience research. We've immersed ourselves in figuring out why healthcare is so complicated in our country, particularly for some of our most vulnerable neighbors.

On many days, it felt like we were drowning. But we discovered that while much of the healthcare system is focused on making profits on products and services, much more is focused on the joys of helping people and serving others. And that's why we wrote this book.

Our Hope for This Book

Our first hope is that this book serves those who serve others. We're hoping to add value to those of you who are frontline clinical care providers—community health workers, nurses, physician assistants, doctors, and more—who, every day, are helping the people who need you most.

We believe your career in healthcare didn't start with you simply wanting a job; instead, taking care of people is in your DNA. We believe you are driven by character and conviction, passion and purpose. We believe that when most healthcare professionals were six or seven, they looked around one day and saw someone—maybe a grandma, mom, dad, uncle, or a teacher—taking care of family, friends, and neighbors, and they quietly said to themselves, "I want to take care of people, too."

But after doing all it took to earn a job caring for people, one day, you realized you were not in *Healthcare* but in the Healthcare *Industry*, with a capital *I*. You want to live your purpose, but you are paid for production instead. As you process thirty or forty patients a day, you can't help but sense that somehow the profits have got to be more important than the people. And it doesn't make sense.

Then, on top of it all, every day, you walk into exam rooms and see patients who don't trust you and your years of education and experience. It's not because of anything you've done but because you are part of a system they don't trust. You feel like there's no flexibility, no agency, and that none of this is turning out how you expected.

We want to help clinicians like yourself put the joy back into your work and to equip and empower you with a tool you can use in your own community.

Our next hope is for this book to enlighten those of you who are healthcare executives, administrators, researchers, and policymakers. Each of you works so hard to understand the ever-changing needs around health in our country, to help make margin match mission, and to somehow balance the needs of a multitude of diverse stakeholders. We want to share stories of success with you, which you can then leverage to improve quality, save money, and change your companies, your communities, and—maybe, if we work together—even our country.

I say that because our final and biggest hope is that our work has a positive impact on the lives of the millions of Americans who, for a variety of reasons, live on the periphery of the traditional healthcare system.

The Mobile Health Model

The mobile health model in the US, as we're using it here, refers to healthcare and human services delivered in mobile medical clinic settings. Not to be confused with mHealth (digital health interventions delivered via mobile phone), these satellite clinics rotate regularly, in a hub-and-spoke path, from their home bases at hospitals or health centers to remote locations, where medical, behavioral, or dental teams provide care directly to hard-to-reach people in hard-to-reach places.

These clinics are equipped with a variety of examination rooms and equipment, offering primary care, preventive services, vaccinations, and various health screenings, such as blood pressure checks, diabetes testing, and cancer screenings. Next-generation clinics offer specialty services, are modular, and have integrated advanced technology.

The patients they typically serve are part of underserved populations: people living in rural areas with limited healthcare access, homeless individuals, migrant workers, and residents of low-income neighborhoods or healthcare deserts.

At its core, the mobile health model reduces the distance between patients and providers and removes transportation and time barriers that prevent people from getting care. It reaches vulnerable populations where they live and work, provides culturally appropriate services in familiar settings, and delivers preventive care in a cost-effective way to people who might otherwise go without medical attention. Critically, it allows for an efficient and effective redistribution of the healthcare workforce that is concentrated in urban and suburban areas out into healthcare deserts.

My father is an example of the millions of Americans who could desperately use a mobile health program in their community today.

And if you're one of the thousands who already work in the mobile health field, know that you have similar values to those my father had, by which you are led to get up, go out, and take care of your neighbor. Those values could be why I am so drawn to this work.

These are the convictions that drive our commitment to mobile health and steer the messages of this book:

- **We believe** mobile health is a great model to deliver healthcare to millions of patients living in rural areas struggling to access healthcare.
- **We believe** mobile health provides an enriching space for providers to work and rest and recuperate, and to rediscover the joy that abounds in helping people understand their bodies and how to care for them.
- **We believe** mobile health is a model that healthcare organizations can leverage to right the ship when it comes to burnout.
- **We believe** mobile health can help restore trust that communities once had in their healthcare systems.

Although the positive outcomes enabled by mobile health are well documented by robust research, we do not believe these things just because the research says so. We believe in mobile health because we see with our eyes the impact this model makes and hear with our ears the stories its champions have told us and feel in our hearts the difference it makes in the lives of people who, above all else, are desperate for someone, anyone, to help them.

The People Driving Mobile Health

When we look closely, we find our country is filled coast-to-coast with medical professionals who are searching for a better way to care for people, particularly the at-risk and underserved patients who need them most, and—in finding the mobile health model—have gone out and made it happen. These professionals not only devote their time on this earth to caring for others but have made the decision to work with at-risk populations, meeting people where they are.

Since founding Mission Mobile Medical Group in 2020, Amanda and I have encountered many of these incredible people, several of whom you are going to learn about in this book.

Mobile health work is not easy. Most days are spent in the field, far away from the nearest air-conditioned office. Working in cramped quarters, spending hours driving around, and parking in pockets of poverty often hidden behind the veil in communities doesn't, at face value, sound like the job of your dreams. To be fair, it's not for everyone.

But for those people and providers who are driven by a need to right wrongs in health equity, who are unbowed by the weight of hard work, it is extraordinarily rewarding. Making a living while making a positive difference in the lives of thousands of your most vulnerable neighbors—what could be better?

Our Road to Mobile Health

As much as my dad loved to help others, he wasn't very good at helping himself. There are a lot of reasons people like my dad don't see a doctor on a regular basis. Some can't afford to, and for many Americans, the doctor's office is an hour away, or a thousand other obstacles. Then again, others could go to the doctor regularly but don't. Some just haven't made medical checkups a regular part of their life. Some find it scary; some are mistrustful.

Growing up in a farm community as I did, you hear things like, "Don't go to the doctor; they'll just find something wrong with you." You see people believing that the doctors are the richest people in town, and some people believe they got that way by finding things wrong with their patients, who are then forced to spend the rest of their lives paying them to fix it.

This is the type of thinking that contributed to my dad's early death. I've heard it said that one of the scariest things to a doctor or nurse is hearing a farmer say he's sick. I believe that because I have a family full of farmers. As a kid, I helped bale hay and muck chicken houses and learned to drive a tractor. I grew up with pastures on three sides of my house, and I still remember how to round up cows that somehow got under the fence.

These are people who work hard every day of their lives. There are no weekends, no quitting time, no sick leave—because there's never an end to the work. It's animals and crops, weather and equipment, plus many mouths to feed. Nature is unkind and the markets unfair most years, and a steady diet of death and unfairness year after year toughens you like nothing else.

And farm families are filled with people who have an "I'm fine" mentality. After all, there's work to do. My father was an always-on worker. And through my mother's people in farming, our family had a mentality of "The work never ends" and "I'm fine." If something bothered my dad, he wouldn't let on. Some might think stoicism is a great strength, but as my friend John always says, "A strength overused becomes a weakness."

My father wasn't a farmer; he was a barber, who, after twenty-five years with hands full of hair and scissors, developed carpal tunnel syndrome, a common condition that occurs when the median nerve in the wrist is compressed and leads to weakness in the hand. He lost the ability to make the fine cuts one must master to maintain a solid reputation as a small-town barber. He saw a doctor, but when they told him surgery was the only fix, he stood up and walked out.

The only time I remember my father going to a hospital was when he had to. Chest pains scared him enough to see a doctor in town, and the only way to stay alive was a quadruple bypass. The scare didn't change him much, and the chain fast-food places he passed every day made it easy to indulge in many less-than-healthy meals.

One morning at work, when he was sixty-six years old and planning his retirement, he had a massive heart attack and died. A customer found him in the back room, alone. He was gone.

In the quiet moments that surrounded the funeral, I found myself sitting alone and comparing the life I was living and the life my father lived. I owned a construction company and was working all over the country on big utility plant contracts and military contracts, even running some renovations on Capitol Hill office buildings in Washington, DC. We were making great money, but the truth was, I was doing all that work, making all that money, for me. And the reality I faced was that it had been years since I'd thought much about anyone else.

I came face-to-face with the cold fact that I wasn't the man my father had raised me to be. And in that moment, I resolved to change. I decided to live the remainder of my life following my father's example and maybe making him proud by carrying on his legacy of being a servant leader who valued all people.

Within six months or so, I had sold our construction business. Amanda and I went back to college to finish our degrees, then bounced around for a while—traveling, teaching overseas, consulting—on the hunt for how to make that decision make a difference. I taught a few courses at the local college, even taking some motivational speaking gigs about my journey. It was a whirlwind, and for years, I didn't have clarity on what I wanted to do.

Then, in 2016, a friend of a friend asked me to lead a turnaround at one of the country's oldest and largest specialty vehicle companies. This company had a storied history and built things such as the Kraft Oscar Mayer Wienermobiles. Over the next few years, things improved, and we landed Fortune 500 clients such as Lockheed Martin, Facebook, Caterpillar Inc., and the US Navy.

In the summer of 2018, a nurse from our local hospital asked us to build a specialty vehicle we'd never built before—a mobile medical clinic. The team drew up a proposal for a custom coach built on a semitruck tractor. I remember it was going to cost over $650,000 and would take over a year to build.

But the more we talked with her and her team, the more I learned that's not how mobile health works. Funds are usually scarce for underserved populations, and big money for fancy mobile clinics with bells and whistles is rare. This was nothing like pitching a national marketing program to another Fortune 500 organization. In fact, it was like nothing I'd ever seen before.

She quickly got to the bottom line: "This grant allows $250,000 for equipment, and we only have until Christmas to get it up and running. What can you do with that?"

Our big, bad custom vehicle idea was no longer an option. Our engineers went back to the drawing board. No one wanted to touch a job with low margins, but after some friction, our team gave me a glimmer of hope. They said that if she would accept an RV shell versus a custom fabricated shell, they could make the money work. It wasn't much of a negotiation. I remember when she said, "If it's out of the sun, out of the rain, and runs every day, it will help these people."

So, I wrote up the contract and invited her team to our office to sign it. And that was the day that changed my life. Many lives, in hindsight.

When clients such as Lockheed Martin, Caterpillar, or Facebook sign a contract, it is a very businesslike process. Procurement negotiates hard, argues over payment terms, checks boxes, and redlines contracts; then, when the deal is done, we would all get up and go to work. There is lots of businesslike handshaking, and some solid slaps on the back for good luck.

When this nurse signed, it was different. She came around the table, and instead of the expected handshake, she gave me a giant hug. I was shocked and remember thinking, *Strange! I've never gotten a hug at work before!* But then, it got better. She pulled away and said, "You'll never know what this is going to mean to the people we're going to see … We're going to take it up in the mountains and see people who don't trust doctors or can't drive the hour into town."

My stomach went into knots because she was wrong. I knew exactly what it would mean to those people, because those were *my* people. I grew up in the Appalachian Mountains. My mom was one of thirteen kids, a big farm family. It was the four-to-a-bed, shoes-once-a-year, no-school-today-because-you're-going-to-hoe-corn type of growing up. When I was little, I ran wild in the woods with cousins and cows and chickens, hunted squirrels and deer and rabbits, and swam in the river. And a thousand times, I heard my parents say, "Get up. We can't afford for you to be sick" and "The hospital is where people go to die." And because of those core beliefs, I believe my parents struggled with their health their entire lives—with obesity, diabetes, and heart disease.

As I stood there, in this hug, I thought of my father and how he died far younger than he should have. Massive heart attack. Only sixty-six, ready to retire. My dad didn't deserve to die that way. In that moment, I thought, "*Wow. What if someone with a heart like this woman had headed up to our little town* and *parked over at the fire department every Tuesday, and maybe met my dad and treated him like a person instead of a profit margin? Would he have lived longer?*

If someone like her had offered my dad a bit of hope for his health, could we have had a few more Christmases together? Would he have met his granddaughter? Maybe he could have finished raising me, at least. Because even at thirty, I wasn't done needing my dad.

And at that moment, like a match to gasoline, whatever spark my dad had planted in me to serve others and to do more and be more burst beautifully into flames. I caught on fire for this work. Now, I believe if we spend our lives helping people help people like my dad—serving those who serve others—our parents will be proud, and we can make this world a better place.

This opportunity was what I had been waiting for. I wanted to work at doing something I loved and to make a real difference in the world. I wanted to help all these people take care of others who were in desperate need, including all the people from where I was born and raised.

What could go wrong?

I started looking at the mobile health space and the competitive landscape and saw some opportunities. I thought this was the direction the owners of our specialty vehicle company should go. There was a growing need for these types of vehicles, and we had a perfect opportunity to lead the industry.

But they didn't like the idea. Or maybe they liked the idea but didn't like me. For whatever reason, right after lunch on the first

Friday of January 2020, they fired me. Frankly, I wasn't surprised. But moreover, I wasn't deterred. As I sat at my desk and listened to the owner's son sitting across from me explain how they didn't need me anymore, I must admit I saw their logic. He was right. They didn't need me. But millions of other people did. I grabbed my bag, said goodbye to my team, and walked out the door into the sunshine.

When I got home, my four-year-old daughter, London, yelled, "Daddy's home!" My wife was a little more subdued; she knew my being home early wasn't normal. I told her what had happened. Her only question was, "What are we going to do?"

She sat in silence as I shared my ideas about mobile health that had been swirling around since that first project and how I felt like we should start a mobile healthcare company. Surprisingly, she liked the idea. Shoulder to shoulder, empowered by our new feeling of purpose, we went to work on our business plan. We incorporated the first week of March 2020. And the next week, the entire country shut down trying to contain COVID-19. What's life without adventure, right?

Startup

It wasn't easy being a medical startup during the biggest pandemic to sweep the globe since the Spanish flu almost exactly one hundred years before.

At least we had people who loved us. Amanda's mom, Jan—a corporate human resource and training executive with experience leading companies such as 7-Eleven and Rita's Italian Ice—relocated from California to Greensboro, moved in with us, and became Mission Mobile teammate number 1.

We cashed in our life insurance and drained our savings account. If anyone wants to test the patience and love your family has for one another, these are the perfect conditions. And as we cranked it up, we cast around for other stars in our little epic adventure and were joined by best friends.

Neil Rotroff, now our VP of Marketing, grew up in San Jose, California, and had a budding career as a world-class industrial designer. But he fell in love with tech and social media engineering and wanted to move to North Carolina to raise his son. We had hired him to my previous team, designing specialty marketing vehicles, and have been close friends ever since. The day I was fired, he walked into my office and said, "That's not cool. Where are we going?" For a guy with very few friends, that's a special thing for me.

Another superstar was Brad Watson. Brad and his wife, Lindsay, joined us early on as partners, and Brad hit the road as our first sales guy. Like with any startup, there was a lot of work to do, and since day one, he has raised his hand for the toughest assignments. I've had four business partners, and I love them all, but Brad is one of the best. I've never once doubted his values, character, work ethic, or integrity, and he has put on a powerful performance taking us to market, with his team driving us over $100 million in revenue before we even hit the five-year mark.

We were small but mighty, and all in on the vision for mobile health.

Being in the middle of a pandemic made it difficult going. Jan worked the phones. One of her projects was to call the governor's office in every state and ask about their plans for vaccinations and how we might help them. We were disappointed to learn that the government and most local health systems had laid plans for natural disasters years before. But Jan was relentless. Sitting at our kitchen table, she would work through page after page of contacts and mazes of prompts and voicemails. When she got someone on the phone, you could hear the excitement in her voice as she explained who we were and that we wanted to help.

As you can guess, a startup calling governors' offices produced zero sales. But we learned a lot, and those months stand as a monument to our reckless optimism and are the foundation of the discipline and diligence found in our organizational culture today: Focus, fight, finish.

There was a lot of learning to do, and education is expensive. Amanda and I had invested everything into making this thing work. And over those first few months, we made zero sales.

Eventually, we bumped the bottom of the barrel. We've always run an open-book operation, and during our Monday morning traffic meeting, Amanda announced to the team that we had $14.87 left in our operating account. Payroll was Friday; we had five days to figure it out.

Our first sale came that week. We had taken a call from a Virginia nonprofit that wanted a mobile health program. Brad and I drove the clinic up to the North Carolina–Virginia border to meet the executive, and at the end of the interview, we walked away with a deposit of $5,000. When I watched Brad stand in our kitchen and hand that check over to Amanda, I felt like a man dying of thirst in the desert who had finally found water.

We needed the money, for sure. But more than that, we needed the energy that came with it. And that's exactly what happened. Our startup mantra had been, "Let's deliver one." It became, "Let's deliver two." Then, "Let's deliver ten." We were on our way.

PART 1

Mobile Health Yesterday

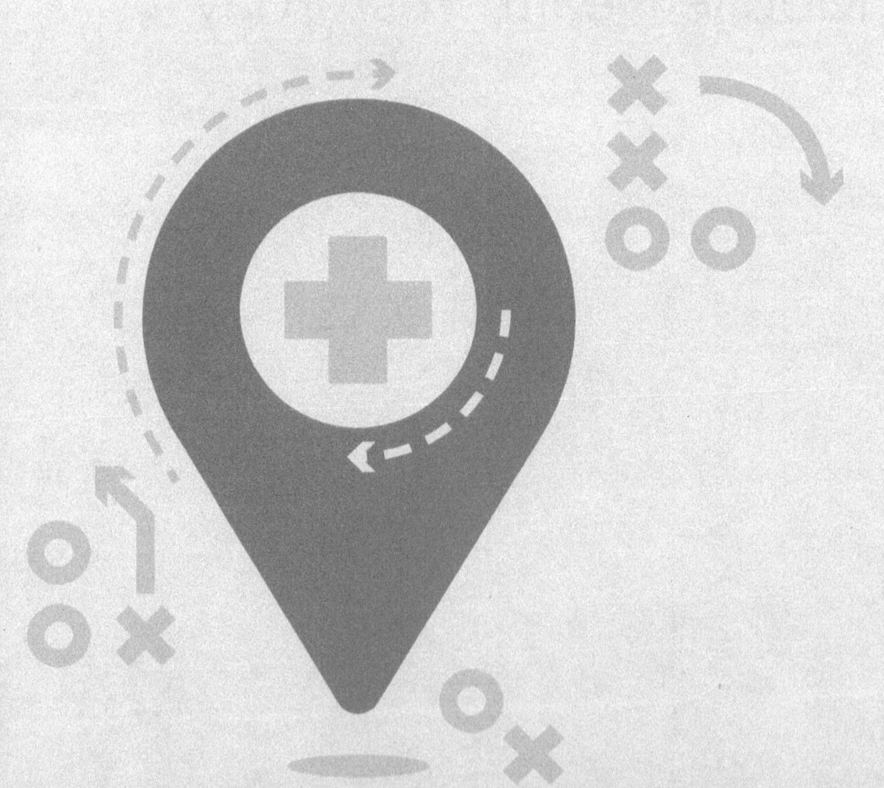

Chapter 1

This Road Has Been Traveled Before

The concept of mobile healthcare is as old as medicine itself. When people are too sick to travel, the doctor gets up and goes to meet them wherever they are.

All over the globe, the phrase "Send for a doctor" is rooted in the fact that there wasn't always a doctor in the small town where people lived, so one would have to come from a bigger town. As doctors regularly rotated between communities on foot, by horseback, then by carriages and cars, mobility was part of medicine. Even within cities, doctors routinely made house calls to patients who, for whatever reason, could not travel to their office. And this mobility often started (and sometimes still starts) before a physician practiced, with many would-be doctors in African, European, and South American countries completing rural rotations during their training.

My family has history here. As you can see in the photo in Figure 1, my great-uncle, Dr. Albert Johnson Eller, traveled by horseback through the mountains of western Wilkes County in North Carolina at the turn of the twentieth century.

"For many years his mode of travel was by horseback, but despite this, he served the people over a large area of western Wilkes County.

To serve as many people as possible, he would travel to an area on a specific day. For example, on Monday to the Stony Fork area, on Tuesday, the Congo area. The people knew his schedule and would leave word for him at key places in the community or homes of critically ill people where they knew he would be visiting.

"At that time there was a considerable amount of typhoid fever and other contagious diseases. He realized the need for and importance of vaccinations to prevent contagious diseases, so when these vaccines became available, he promoted, encouraged, and administered them. Mrs. (Nancy) Eller learned how to administer some of these vaccines and was a big help with the program.

"The closest dentist was in North Wilkesboro, thirteen miles away, so he pulled a lot of teeth. Mrs. Eller helped him. So many came to his office and home that she began to pull teeth. For years she pulled more aching teeth than he did. With drug stores thirteen miles away, it was necessary for him to keep a supply of medicine in his office and to carry a supply in his saddlebags as he visited patients."[5]

Figure 1. Source: Wilkes County Genealogical Society

5 *The Ellers of Wilkes County, NC* (Eller Family Association, 1993), https://www.ellerfamilyassociation.com/research/Ellers_of_Wikes_Co.pdf.

That was yesterday. When people couldn't get to the doctor, they expected their doctor to come to them. The hill we're climbing today isn't new terrain but a revival, a renewal of how healthcare used to be distributed to everyone in need.

When Doctors Wrote Prescriptions for Food

Fast-forward to the 1960s, and we find a mobile health pioneer in Dr. H. Jack Geiger, who was well known for his commonsense prescription that drove government officials crazy.

When patients came to his clinic malnourished and desperate, the prescription he wrote for them said something revolutionary: "Food." In a 2016 interview, Dr. Geiger described what happened next: "The governor of Mississippi screamed at someone in the poverty program, who came down and screamed at me. 'What in God's name do you think you're doing giving away free food and charging it to the pharmacy? A pharmacy is for drugs to treat a disease.' And I said, 'The last time I looked at my textbooks, the most specific therapy for malnutrition was food.' And so, he went away because he couldn't think of anything to say to that."[6]

Dr. Geiger saw what my father's generation lived with: a healthcare system that operated from ivory towers instead of meeting people where they were. And he understood that you can't treat disease without also treating its root causes, such as hunger. Born and raised in New York City, surrounded by artists and deep thinkers, he was a passionate advocate who decided to do something about these problems.

---

6 H. Jack Geiger, "A Public Health Pioneer," interview by Bill Lubinger, *Think Magazine*, Case Western Reserve University, Spring 2016, https://case.edu/think/spring2016/public-health-pioneer.html.

During the height of the 1960s civil rights movement, Dr. Geiger headed to Mississippi for Freedom Summer. He brought with him a radically innovative model of healthcare he'd encountered as a visiting medical student in South Africa, where doctors worked directly in communities, addressing not just medical needs but also the social conditions that made people sick. Alongside Dr. Count Gibson and Dr. John Hatch, Dr. Geiger built a clinic in Mound Bayou, Mississippi, where they didn't just treat the sick but also dug wells, created libraries, and provided educational and financial services. They understood that health starts where you live, learn, work, and pray.

Dr. Hatch described what they were up against: Physicians across Mississippi, both Black and white, worried the health centers would reduce their patient base.

"There was a lot of radical rhetoric around citizen participation, but nobody quite knew what that meant. Are we really going to let people who can't read and write sit up and make decisions about healthcare? Eventually, the answer was: Yes. And we put together over time and with mistakes, groups of people who certainly enhanced the targeting and appropriateness of things that we did. Another way to look at it, it was very closely akin to theories I read about an economic development process where tasks were viewed from the perspective of what part of this could we develop local talent? How much education do you really need to be a nursing assistant? How could we get professional organizations and societies to respect the new kinds of professionals that we propose to develop?"[7]

Dr. Geiger saw that community health workers, nursing assistants, and community outreach workers didn't need medical degrees

7 H. Jack Geiger, foreword to *Out in the Rural: A Mississippi Health Center and Its War on Poverty*, by Thomas J. Ward Jr. (Oxford University Press, 2017).

to make a profound difference. They needed training, support, and respect. Most importantly, they needed to be from the communities they served. When you train local talent and invest in community members, you create economic opportunity alongside healthcare access. He also knew that patients play an important role because they know better than anyone what they need, just as communities understand their own challenges better than distant bureaucrats.

"Part of my job was to discuss options and perspectives. Hopes and dreams. And encourage local people to participate because initially, the response was, 'Are you crazy? Are you going to really turn this over to a group of people who might struggle with language and expression?' Of course, the answer was yes."[8]

Dr. Geiger wrote: "Because poor healthcare and poor health so profoundly limit opportunities for the full realization of one's potential, justice in healthcare is good for the public's health, and the public's good health, in turn, broadens opportunities and facilitates a more just society."[9]

The clinic in Mississippi, along with one Dr. Geiger founded in Boston's Columbia Point housing project, became the models for a nationwide movement. By 2024, there were more than 1,500 community health centers around the country. What I admire most about Dr. Geiger's story is his emphasis on dignity and seeing people as whole human beings, not just a collection of symptoms.

8 ibid.

9 ibid.

Stepping Outside to Talk to People: Dr. Nancy Oriol

To understand how we got where we are today in mobile health, you will want to know Dr. Nancy Oriol, former dean of students at Harvard Medical School and founder of Mobile Health Map.

Dr. Oriol launched mobile healthcare in its current form. And for more than three decades, she's been fighting this fight, proving that servant leadership in healthcare isn't just good medicine but is also smart business.

This work, and supporting the people doing it, was Dr. Oriol's passion and purpose long before it was mine. She has taken what some might view as charity work and turned it into an area of academic and economic study within the healthcare community.

One of the tenets of her philosophy is that mobile health works because it is so flexible. Flexibility is not only about location and all the places a clinician can meet people, but also about how a program can provide precisely the services a community needs, exactly when they need them. Here's Dr. Oriol's story, in her own words:

"It was 1992. I was working at Harvard when *The Boston Globe* ran this devastating seven-part series called The Death Zone. Right here in the shadows of Harvard Medical School and world-class hospitals, infant mortality rates among minorities were worse than in Third World countries.

I had three young children at the time. Everyone kept saying it was all about prenatal care—either people didn't know how to get it or couldn't afford it. But I knew that wasn't the whole story. Prenatal care is simple: check urine, check blood pressure. Black bears have the lowest infant mortality rate of any mammal, and they don't have prenatal care.

Then came my origin story—the case that changed everything. A pregnant woman arrived at our hospital unconscious. We did an emergency C-section because the baby was in distress. After she woke up, I asked what happened. She'd had a terrible headache for days but didn't want to bother her doctor. She was afraid of looking stupid.

She had insurance. She had access. What she didn't have was understanding. She didn't know that headaches are a sign of pre-eclampsia—a condition that can kill you and your baby.

Just before this, I'd treated another pregnant woman with the exact same condition. But she was from a wealthy neighborhood. She came in early, stayed a few weeks, and had close monitoring. She and her baby did fine.

Same condition. Two completely different outcomes. The difference wasn't money or insurance. It was knowledge and access to someone who cared enough to explain things in a way she could understand."

Dr. Oriol could have written a research paper about health disparities. But instead, she did something unexpected, and, in hindsight, revolutionary: She took her stethoscope and walked outside.

"I didn't go out there as a person from Harvard trying to tell people how to do things. I went out there and asked questions. I talked to ministers, to guys in barbershops, to anyone who would listen. I asked what they thought the problem was, what the solution could be."

That's how The Family Van was born. Dr. Oriol and medical student Cheryl Dorsey started with a refurbished van parked a few blocks from Massachusetts General Hospital, caring for people who couldn't or wouldn't go inside. The program still exists on the streets of Boston. As they described it, they discovered that "health starts where you live, learn, work, and pray. We must reach out, be in the neighborhood, and meet people where they are."

The results spoke for themselves. One man came in for a diabetes screening but had dangerously high blood pressure. They sent him straight to the hospital, where doctors discovered his heart was a ticking time bomb. He would have had a stroke or died within days. Another patient's routine screening caught cancer early. Seven years later, he's still in remission.

Dr. Oriol understood that this wasn't just about medical care but also about earning trust. Research showed that people from challenged lifestyles were more likely to use The Family Van because they felt safe in their neighborhoods, away from the judgment they feared in traditional medical offices.

Dr. Oriol wasn't the first to recognize this trust problem. In 1966, Martin Luther King Jr. called out the American Medical Association for its "conspiracy of inaction" in providing proper medical care to minorities. He said, "Of all the forms of inequality, injustice in health is the most shocking and the most inhuman because it often results in physical death."[10]

Today, Dr. Oriol's team at Mobile Health Map, including the executive director, Mary Kathryn Fallon, tracks more than 1,300 mobile medical clinics around the country. What started as one van in Boston has become a movement. Dr. Oriol created a legacy that extends far beyond her own work.

When we first learned about Dr. Oriol's journey, we realized we weren't alone on this road. Dr. Oriol had been climbing this hill for decades, proving it could be done, showing the rest of us the way. In fact, in our conversations for this book, this overlap in our stories struck a nerve for her. She is from a Jamaican family that had

10 "Dr. Martin Luther King on Health Care Injustice," Physicians for a National Health Program, https://pnhp.org/news/dr-martin-luther-king-on-health-care-injustice/.

immigrated to the United States, and her father had also suffered from both fear of medical care and lack of access to it.

"My dad died early because he didn't have time to go to the doctor, and he didn't believe in going to the doctor, which is ironic," Dr. Oriol said. "He would complain all the time about having a charley horse. He'd wrap it up all the time.

"He also worked so much. He got a second job when I was in my first year in college. What he didn't learn is that a charley horse is a sign of blood clots, and he ended up having a seizure and died of a stroke. I was nineteen years old and an undergraduate at Boston University. It was an early indication to me of how difficult it was for the working poor to get proper care."

Dr. Geiger and Dr. Oriol exemplify the best of transforming direct, personal experiences into action. They are among the early leaders we at Mission Mobile Medical admire, respect, and feel immense gratitude toward for the path they have paved. In the next chapter, I'll tell you about another leader who has made tremendous inroads in bringing mobile health where it is needed.

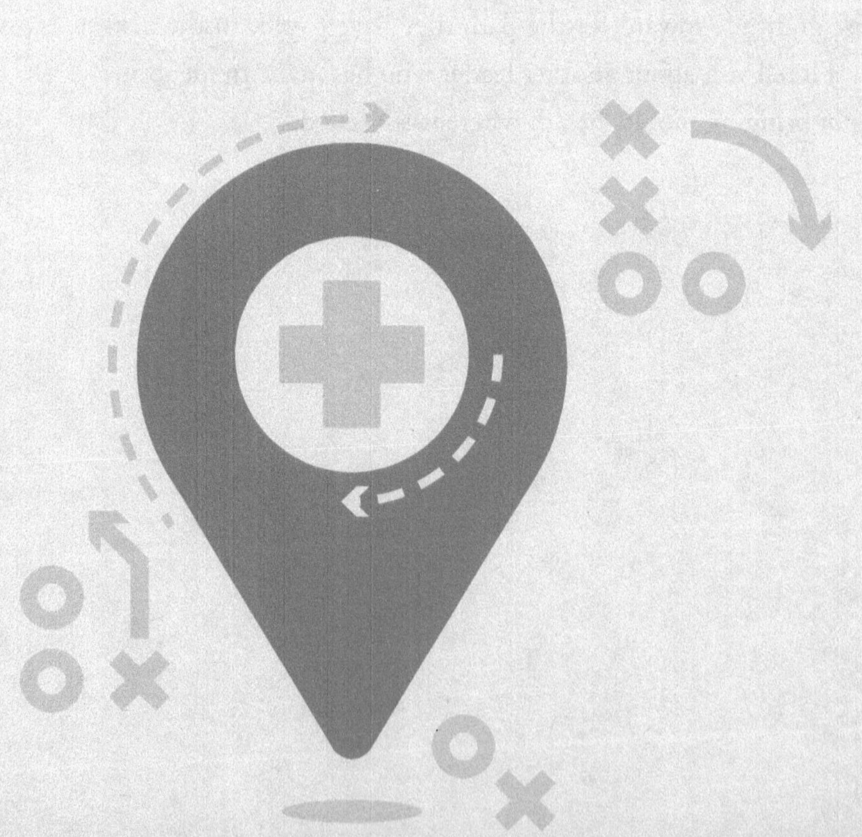

Chapter 2
The Bridge Builder

Dr. Kyu Rhee asks the tough questions. As CEO of the National Association of Community Health Centers, he's seen healthcare from every angle—bedside to boardroom, clinic to Capitol Hill. When I tell him about the promise and potential we see in having mobile health programs in every county in the country, he doesn't just nod and smile. He peppers me with questions: How are these programs paid for? How are they sustainable? How do we maintain standards? How do we improve them over time? How do they address health equity?

Dr. Rhee brings a unique perspective to this conversation. His mother was a nurse, his father an economist. Both were immigrants who came to America and mapped out a successful future for their family. From his mother, he learned the clinical side—direct patient care, health systems thinking. From his father, he learned to see the bigger picture, to understand the economics that make or break healthcare programs.

"I come at this from a different perspective," he said. "I've worked in the nonprofit, the public, and the private sectors. I've been a primary care doctor, a chief medical officer, and now CEO. So, some of these questions are from just being in it."

Being in it has taught him something crucial: There's a difference between healthcare equity and health equity. It's not just semantics—it's the difference between treating disease and preventing it, between fixing problems and addressing root causes.

"Healthcare equity is predominantly about clinical issues," Dr. Rhee explained. "As a doctor, I learn skills to diagnose disease, to treat that disease, to prescribe drugs and treatments. But health equity goes beyond the exam room. It goes into social drivers of health—transportation, housing, education, food, health deserts."

This sounds familiar. It's the same insight Dr. Geiger had when he wrote prescriptions for food. It's what Dr. Oriol discovered when she took her stethoscope to the street. Health starts where you live, learn, work, and pray.

But Dr. Rhee sees something else: mobile health as a bridge. "The beauty of mobile health is reversing the paradigm," he said. "Instead of expecting people to come to us, we take responsibility to go where people are. We have the humility to understand that we have a responsibility to meet people where they are."

From this perspective, mobile health is going upstream of the emergency department (ED) and catching conditions before they become crises. One-third of people with diabetes and hypertension don't get their condition detected until later stages.[11,12] They don't see a doctor until they're feeling symptoms—problems with sight, lesions that won't heal, or frequent urination at night.

---

11 Institute for Health Metrics and Evaluation, "New Study: Nearly Half of Those with Diabetes Unaware They Have the Disease," news release, September 8, 2025, https://www.healthdata.org/news-events/newsroom/news-releases/new-study-nearly-half-those-diabetes-unaware-they-have-disease.

12 World Health Organization, "Hypertension," fact sheet, September 25, 2025, https://www.who.int/news-room/fact-sheets/detail/hypertension.

"These are signs of diabetes," Dr. Rhee explained. "Diabetes is the number one cause of blindness, the number one cause of amputations, the number one cause of kidney failure. With hypertension, you have a stroke, but you've had undetected hypertension probably decades before that stroke happens."

Mobile health can change this equation. Instead of waiting for people to get sick enough to seek care, mobile units can park next to churches, barber shops, grocery stores—places where communities congregate. They can screen people early, get them into the healthcare system, address chronic conditions before they become life-threatening.

"We need mobile health programs to connect with and serve those communities," Dr. Rhee said, "to screen people early, to get them into the healthcare system. These teams can provide care not just for special-risk populations like the homeless, but for so many settings where the community congregates."

What we appreciate most about Dr. Rhee's perspective is that he doesn't just see the promise; he tackles practical challenges head-on. There are billing issues in some parts of the country. There are productivity standards clinicians must meet. There is a real need that billable hours justify compensation. These aren't just administrative details—they're the difference between sustainable programs and well-intentioned failures.

His biggest question cuts to the heart of everything: "As a community health center, how are we best using the mobile health model to effectively introduce patients to providers and overcome the lack of trust that sometimes exists?"

Trust. There it is again. The same issue Dr. Oriol discovered in Boston, and the same problem Dr. Geiger faced in Mississippi. Whether you're dealing with urban communities that have been failed by the system or rural communities that feel forgotten by it, trust is the foundation everything else is built on.

Dr. Rhee understands this because he's been building trust for years. Community health centers serve nearly thirty-four million patients annually (more than one in ten Americans) while representing only 1 percent of total healthcare spending.[13] They've proven that when you go into underserved communities, when you provide comprehensive care regardless of ability to pay, when you focus on health equity rather than just healthcare equity—lives change.

Mobile health isn't replacing this work—it's extending it. It's taking the proven model of community health centers and making it even more accessible, even more responsive to exactly what people need.

Dr. Rhee sees mobile health as part of the solution, but he also sees it clearly. The resources must be there. The framework must be holistic. The care must be comprehensive. And most importantly, the trust must be real.

Servant leaders at community health centers across our country and out in our territories, such as Dr. Rhee, have been fighting this fight for decades, building bridges between communities and care—proving that when you meet people where they are with what they need, healing happens.

The question isn't whether mobile health works; it's whether we're ready to build it right, sustain it properly, and earn the trust it requires.

The bridge between patients and providers is built. Now, we must all cross it.

---

13 "America's Health Centers: By the Numbers," National Association of Community Health Centers, January 9, 2026, www.nachc.org/resource/americas-health-centers-by-the-numbers/.

Chapter 3

"Take a Ride with Me"

Dr. Kyu Rhee wanted me to know about a legend. "She was an amazing woman," he said. "I spent time with her at Christ House and in a mobile van serving the unhoused. She showed me what it really means to go where people are."

Her name was Dr. Janelle Goetcheus, and she was known as the Mother Teresa of Washington, DC. For nearly fifty years, she cared for the underprivileged, the homeless, and the poor. From drug addicts to the disabled, she cared for anyone and everyone she could reach.

But Dr. Goetcheus didn't just treat patients and send them home. She moved her family into the facility where she cared for the homeless. When Christ House opened in 1985 as a thirty-seven-bed facility for homeless people dealing with severe illnesses, Dr. Goetcheus and her husband, Reverend Allen Goetcheus, moved in and raised their family there.

"We wanted to learn to be with people and not just to do for people," Dr. Goetcheus explained in an oral history interview.[14]

---

14 Janelle Goetcheus, "Interview with Janelle Goetcheus," interview by Dave Long, Christ House, May 6, 2015, audio, christhouse.org/interview-with-janelle-goetcheus/.

It was a tremendous show of generosity, but as she admitted, it put tremendous strain on her children. Their lives were a challenge, as they dealt with growing up in the rough Adams Morgan neighborhood where Christ House was located. "My children felt a lot of anger," she told *The New York Times Magazine* in 1986. "They were brought into the city, mugged on the street, and had their stuff stolen."[15]

Dr. Goetcheus persevered. She had to. She had seen too much to turn back.

One of my favorite stories about Dr. Goetcheus, published in her *Wall Street Journal* obituary, tells of a winter night when she and her colleagues approached a group of men struggling to stay warm around a steam grate during the holidays. The group shivered in the shadow of the White House as tourists milled about, visiting the National Christmas Tree, ignoring their plight.

"One had infected burns. Another had pneumonia. A third, they soon learned, had laryngeal cancer. Around them were tourists visiting the nation's capital, and Goetcheus could see the lights of the National Christmas Tree. It felt wrong."[16]

Dr. Goetcheus was, in her own way, an original mobile healthcare provider. She was grounded in faith, Midwestern values, and a love of the underdog story.

"People who are in Christian ministry their whole lives say Janelle was the most Christ-like person that they've met," Dr. Cheryl Watts told *The Washington Post*.

Charles Barber, whose father, Dr. Jesse Barber (one of the nation's first Black neurosurgeons), helped co-found Christ House, put it this way: "Dr. Goetcheus is the embodiment of the teachings of Matthew

15 Janelle Goetcheus, interview, *The New York Times Magazine*, 1986.

16 Harry Jaffe, "Janelle Goetcheus, Physician and Healer to D.C.'s Homeless, Dies at 84," *The Washington Post*, November 11, 2024, www.washingtonpost.com/obituaries/2024/11/11/janelle-goetcheus-homeless-doctor-dead/.

25: 'When I was hungry, and you gave me something to eat, I was thirsty and you gave me something to drink, I was a stranger and you invited me in, I needed clothes and you clothed me, I was sick and you looked after me, I was in prison and you came to visit me.'"

Even as she battled cancer toward the end of her life, Dr. Goetcheus put the emphasis on caring for others. Ray Maun met her in 2021 when he was sixty-one, homeless, and dealing with diabetes and drug addiction. Dr. Goetcheus said to him, simply and elegantly, "Take a ride with me."

He did. She got him enrolled at Christ House, where he stayed for several months. He relapsed and overdosed on fentanyl before returning to Christ House. He eventually got sober, moved to Kairos House (another facility Dr. Goetcheus helped found), and eventually rented his own apartment. He reconnected with his family, including his grandchildren.

"The whole thing goes back to Dr. Goetcheus," Maun told *The Washington Post*. "All this started with her saying: 'Come take a ride with me.'"

When people asked Dr. Goetcheus about those who see the homeless as an eyesore, she had a gentle but firm response: "Those who see a homeless person as an 'eyesore' probably have not had time to get to know them as individuals or had the opportunity to hear that person's story. Not knowing them as persons, who they are, or their giftedness is only due to a lack of significant contact."

Dr. Goetcheus broke down the barriers between doctors and patients—barriers that are often mental walls, not literal ones. She did it through force of will and willingness to sacrifice. She did it by moving her family into the solution. She did it by saying, "Take a ride with me."

That's mobile health at its purest—not just bringing medicine to people but bringing yourself. Not just treating symptoms but seeing the whole person. Not just providing care but providing dignity.

Dr. Goetcheus inspired hundreds of other doctors to follow her example, including Dr. Kyu Rhee, who worked alongside her serving the unhoused. She showed them what it really means to meet people where they are.

Our country has tens of thousands of doctors, nurses, and other clinicians with the desire, talent, mindset, and skill set to solve society's biggest healthcare challenges. Dr. Goetcheus showed us what's possible when we give people with compassion the tools and systemic support to do so.

The hill we're climbing isn't just about better healthcare delivery. It's about saying to the forgotten, the overlooked, the abandoned, "Come take a ride with me."

We're not alone on this journey. Dr. Goetcheus walked this path before us, showing us that the road to healing often starts with a simple invitation.

Chapter 4

Here We Are

History has brought us to this moment. And frankly, when you look at healthcare in our country, it's not a pretty picture.

We've built a system unlike the one Dr. Geiger, Dr. Oriol, and Dr. Goetcheus envisioned. They saw patients as whole human beings, when some simply see billing codes and reimbursement rates. Where they wrote prescriptions for food and hope, others process patients and write prescriptions to generate profits. While they moved out into communities and knocked on doors, today, many organizations build fortress-like medical centers that require appointments scheduled weeks or months in advance.

Modern medicine in the US has, in many ways, turned away from purpose and people and toward productivity and profit. And the results are telling.

Nearly one in three Americans delays or skips care because of cost.[17] Medical debt is the leading cause of personal bankruptcy.[18] By 2034, the US could face a shortfall of up to 124,000 physicians[19] and hundreds of thousands of nurses.[20] Even before COVID-19, roughly 40 percent of physicians and nurses reported burnout.[21]

Care remains siloed. Data rarely travels smoothly. Patients with multiple chronic conditions—four in ten adults!—navigate a maze of portals, referrals, and coverage rules.[22] Black mothers die of pregnancy-related causes at three times the rate of White mothers.[23]

Like me, you may have asked yourself, "What have we become?"

My friend John Maxwell says, "Everything rises and falls on leadership." And one of the subtle issues with healthcare access is the hierarchical nature of communication in the medical profession.

---

17 Grace Sparks et al., "Americans' Challenges with Health Care Costs," *KFF*, December 11, 2025, www.kff.org/health-costs/americans-challenges-with-health-care-costs/.

18 David U. Himmelstein et al., "Medical Bankruptcy: Still Common Despite the Affordable Care Act," *American Journal of Public Health* 109, no. 3 (2019): 431–33, doi.org/10.2105/ajph.2018.304901.

19 Association of American Medical Colleges, *The Complexities of Physician Supply and Demand: Projections From 2019 to 2034* (AAMC, 2024), www.aamc.org/media/75231/download.

20 Gretchen Berlin et al., "Assessing the Lingering Impact of COVID-19 on the Nursing Workforce," *McKinsey & Company*, May 11, 2022, www.mckinsey.com/industries/healthcare/our-insights/assessing-the-lingering-impact-of-covid-19-on-the-nursing-workforce.

21 Martha Hostetter and Sarah Klein, "Transforming Care: Responding to Burnout and Moral Injury Among Clinicians," *The Commonwealth Fund*, August 17, 2023, www.commonwealthfund.org/publications/2023/aug/responding-burnout-and-moral-injury-among-clinicians.

22 "Chronic Diseases in America," Centers for Disease Control and Prevention, last updated December 13, 2022, https://stacks.cdc.gov/view/cdc/61396.

23 "Working Together to Reduce Black Maternal Mortality," Centers for Disease Control and Prevention, April 8, 2024, www.cdc.gov/womens-health/features/maternal-mortality.html.

"Medicine is very hierarchical," said Dr. Kyu Rhee. "It has many similarities to the military and the clergy. I would argue it's as simple as the term *patient*. You're categorized and, essentially, told to stay in a waiting room. We expect people to come to us and wait for us."

There are good reasons for medical hierarchy—life-and-death decisions require clear orders and instructions. But the language that goes with hierarchy can stifle communication between healthcare professionals trying to deliver information and patients trying to understand it.

Communication is hard. It's like going to a foreign country and not speaking the language. You don't order the exact food you want. You don't buy the exact item you need. You don't even know how to ask.

There's a reason Hollywood popularized the expression, "Give it to me straight, Doc." It was a direct acknowledgement that patients often don't understand what they're being told. They want doctors to cut through the gobbledygook.

Almost daily in medical forums, we see providers asking each other, "What do I do with patients who don't follow my advice?" Immediately following is a parade of finger-pointers castigating patients as irresponsible. "You can't want them to be healthy more than they want to be healthy!" "All I can do is tell them! The rest is up to them!" "I give them the pill! If they don't take it, that's their own fault!"

There's fierce resentment that when a patient doesn't stay healthy or doesn't understand why treatment is important, it's just their own fault, a personal failing.

I've yet to see a provider take responsibility for their communication skills and say, "You know, this lack of results tells me I am communicating but there's no understanding. What do I need to change about my style or delivery or content to get them to understand?"

My grandma always said, "Honey, when you point your finger at someone else, never forget there are three more pointing back at you." What if kindergarten teachers said, "All I can do is show them the book! I can't learn it for them! You know, we just can't let it bother us when these kids can't read!"

Communication is the responsibility of the communicator, not the audience. Taking responsibility is the role of the leader—the person who has been gifted the advantages in life, who is talented in the subject matter, who understands the material. Leaders take responsibility for themselves and for those in their charge.

We've seen what happens when doctors such as Geiger, Oriol, and Goetcheus decide to meet people where they are instead of expecting them to come to us.

The hill is steep, but the path has been blazed by giants who came before us. The question isn't whether we can climb this hill—it's whether we have the courage to follow their example.

The road back to caring healthcare starts with a simple decision: Are we going to keep pointing fingers at patients who don't understand us, or are we going to change how we communicate? Are we going to keep expecting people to come to us, or are we going to go where they are?

Yesterday's doctors knew the answer. America's health tomorrow depends largely on whether we remember it.

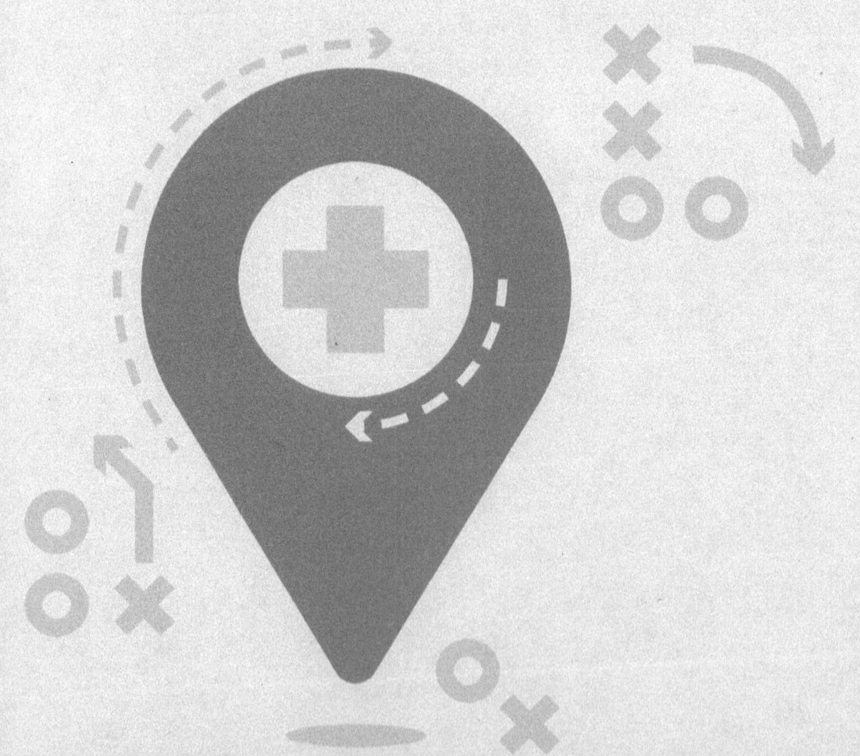

PART 2

Mobile Health Today

Chapter 5

Mobile Health at a Crossroads

The reality is that, today, most mobile health programs are primarily used for education and outreach, indigent care, and—when the sun shines—parades and health fairs.

We've dropped the ball on the potential impact this model might have on health and wellness. Maybe we're hoping AI saves us, or maybe that some new digital tool or virtual tracking can take the place of robust in-person primary care. The data doesn't support that hope. And if you have a mom or dad, they likely feel the same way my parents felt about technology—a little scared.

The good news is that the mobile health model has attracted some transformational leaders, and they are beginning to create networks of satellite mobile health clinics that work together across agencies and health systems to turn the tide and rapidly, significantly, and sustainably deliver improvements in health outcomes.

This matters because more than eighty million Americans—our most vulnerable neighbors—live in areas without adequate healthcare providers.[24] For forty-plus years now, mobile clinics have been a way to extend the reach of healthcare infrastructure to communities where people cannot or will not drive sixty or even thirty minutes to a doctor's office. Or, in some cases, who don't understand or trust the healthcare system for anything other than emergent care.

But here's the problem: Grants are typically used for providers and research institutions to purchase vehicles outright, as in buying a car. And since there is no "standard" model for mobile health, today's mobile health units are mostly built as custom specialty vehicles. The result is that healthcare professionals with little to no experience operating or maintaining a special vehicle suddenly find themselves responsible for the utilization of a big and complicated machine. When that machine breaks, no system for service exists for repairs. No repairability = no reliability.

In today's paradigm, three other realities exist:

1. Financial leverage is inherently limited; every single use case requires a single dedicated chassis. Medical care? Buy a clinic. Dental care? Buy another clinic. Behavioral health? Buy another clinic.

2. The chassis component (which costs between $100,000 and $200,000) becomes "captured capital." The return is severely limited to a certain number of visits for a single clinical use case in a single geography.

3. Minor mechanical issues regularly interrupt scheduled programming: In our experience, many practitioners allow staff to treat a mobile clinic like a teenager treats their car—drive

24 "Closing the Primary Care Gap: How Community Health Centers Can Address the Nation's Primary Care Crisis," National Association of Community Health Centers, February 7, 2023, https://www.nachc.org/resource/closing-the-primary-care-gap-how-community-health-centers-can-address-the-nations-primary-care-crisis/.

> it until it doesn't work. "What's that blinking light?" "Oh, it's been on for months!" Even organizations with fleet managers don't often understand components unique to mobile clinics, such as generator engines, onboard HVAC systems, hydraulic slides, and battery and waste systems.

Manufacturers of mobile clinics, like most companies built to manufacture products, believe their responsibility ends at product delivery. Since entering this field, I have seen many manufacturers take advantage of unsophisticated buyers, delivering subpar products while providing zero support for service or programming, and then wiggling away from their warranty responsibilities. You would think that wouldn't be sustainable, but because most nonprofits aren't litigious, it is. They eat the losses rather than enforce their rights through litigation.

The result is that most new mobile clinic programs in the US flounder. And when they flounder, organizations talk to each other about the failure. Human nature leads to blaming outsiders—vendors, consultants, or prior management. The result is that most healthcare systems have a perception that the risk of expanding access to care via mobile medicine outweighs the promise.

That perception is preventing uptake and expansion of the model.

But for those who think we can't create a system to deliver care to every corner of the 3,143 counties and parishes in the country, consider that the US has, at this very moment, a critical safety net of 52,288 fire stations. Most are not complicated—cinder-block bays, donated gear, and a fire engine. And precisely when the need arises, each fills with men and women heeding the call for help from their neighbors.

The fire station model is an example of dynamic distribution. Driven by data analysis and GIS mapping, our nation has ensured that a large majority of US residents are within a relatively short distance, often within ten minutes, of a fire station.

Public health professionals should take note. There is broad recognition that primary care should play a more central role in healthcare, and that efficient distribution of primary care improves outcomes and reduces costs. The effects of expanding access to care are well studied and long accepted.

The reality to confront is that when people believe they have an urgent health concern, and they cannot get attention from physicians or specialists in a timely manner, they have proven they will turn to EDs, where all stakeholders incur significantly higher costs.

The latest mobile health models mirror our fire service: simple infrastructure built in partnership with community leaders, predictive modeling to identify need, and efficient distribution of resources. Networks of satellite mobile health clinics rotate care teams through rural communities on regular schedules.

Backed by technology supporting predictive cost savings and dynamic resource allocation, this model can ensure healthcare professionals are positioned precisely where and when communities need them.

This approach reduces transportation barriers, promotes primary care utilization, and has the potential to significantly improve outcomes and lower the total cost of care, producing rapid, significant, and sustainable improvements.

But we can't forget the people. There are those who are out in the world doing this work today.

In the next few chapters, I'm going to introduce you to people who are empathetic and care about others and discuss how they are tackling this work. And I'm also going to introduce you to a population you may or may not be familiar with—people who live on the margins, who have very tough lives and big problems.

The reality public health professionals must face is that most people are just trying to make it through the day. Many are living dangerously close to the poverty line. They don't have time to educate themselves on the hot button issue of the day or the latest medical research; they're just trying to keep it together.

If we want to help them, we are compelled to do two things: (1) go out and find them, and (2) show them how we are going to help them.

When I say *find* them, I mean literally go where they are. Not wait for them to come to us. Not send them appointment reminders they can't keep. Not assume they know we exist and they could come if they wanted to. Go to the apartment complex. Go to the trailer parks. Go to the grocery stores. Go to the churches and community centers. Go to the places where people gather, where they already trust their leaders, where they already feel safe.

When I say *show* them, I don't mean tell them about all the wonderful services we provide. I don't mean more marketing flyers or Facebook posts. I mean demonstrate, right there on the spot, how we're going to make their life better. Connect with them as human beings. Check their blood pressure. Give them a box of Band-Aids or socks. Ask them about their feelings, their fears of what this number might mean. Give them relief, something tangible they can take home. Prove that you're not just another person with a clipboard telling them what to do.

And when I say help *them*, I mean focus on the individual person standing in front of you, not the population health statistics on your dashboard. We must have clarity and create a direct line of sight between what we see as a clinician versus what matters most to them.

To be clear, this is not "*We're* going to improve health in this community." This is "Let's relieve *your* pain, make *you* feel better, so you can enjoy *your* life more and be around longer for *your* family."

Learning to talk in terms of the other person's interests is a simple mental pivot lost on most professionals, but one which makes all the difference when communicating with stressed-out people in survival mode. They just want to know, "How are you going to make *my* life better?" And it's not selfish; it's survival. It's not their fault; it's a reaction to their environment.

We must adjust our thinking and behavior to accommodate the person we're there to help. Caring for others is about more than just providing procedures. Sometimes it takes critical thinking and questioning our own beliefs about how things should be done.

Like learning to play the piano, achieving above-average results usually takes above-average effort. If we ever want a shot at digging ourselves out of this healthcare hole, we must take the lead and go where people are. That will take prioritization of the important over the urgent, discipline, scoreboards, and creating a cadence of accountability with our stakeholders.

Numbers are nothing more than shadows of people. These communities aren't a monolith of impossibly hard-to-reach people. A chunk of them might need a reminder about their checkups, but some will need to be shown there's something to live for. We will likely need to share that message in multiple languages.

Dr. Geiger understood this when he wrote prescriptions for food. Dr. Oriol understood this when she took her stethoscope to the street. Dr. Goetcheus understood this when she said, "Take a ride with me."

They knew that healthcare isn't really about systems and policies and quality metrics. It's about people. Real people with real problems who need real help.

In the next chapters, I will introduce you to some of the most powerful people I know. And as I do that, I'm betting you will hear a voice—not in your head but in your heart—asking, "What about me? Am I willing to answer the call?"

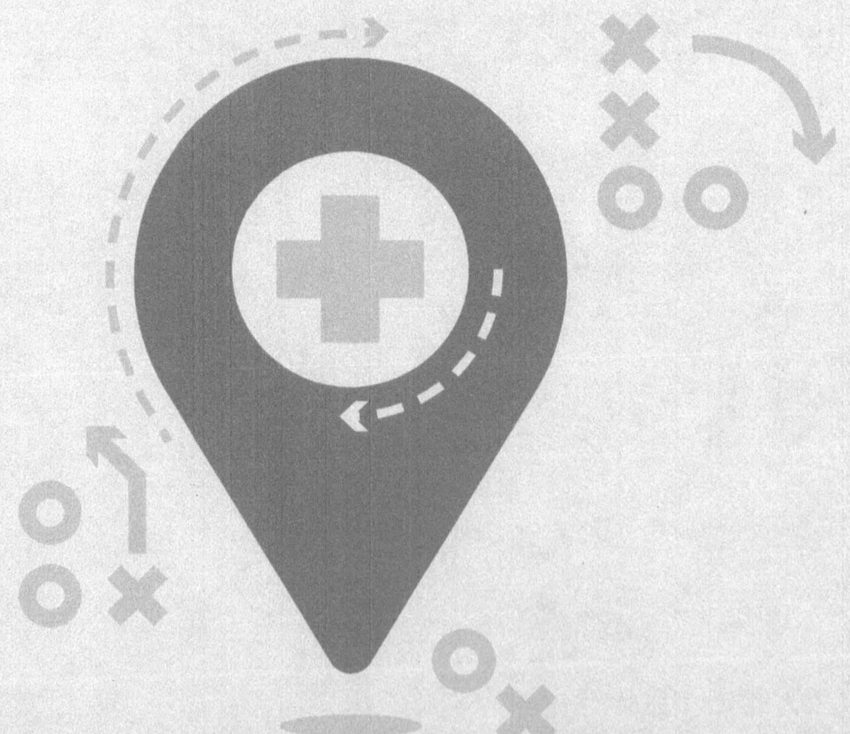

Chapter 6

"No Bueno"

Jose Juarez is a migrant farmworker who lives with his wife and three children outside of Los Banos, California, the land made famous in song and literature by everyone from Woody Guthrie to John Steinbeck.

Juarez and his wife, now in their early thirties, have been together since they were teenagers. And although he uses the word *wife*, they are not legally married because, you know … "paperwork." They are joined in all the other ways: by love, by children, and now cemented by responsibility to the family and life they have created. Juarez struggles to keep his family above the poverty line.

His responsibilities lead Juarez and his twenty-year-old Ford Bronco all over the Central Valley. He often drives up and over distant Mount Diablo and into the lush farmland along California's Pacific Coast. By his own definition, Juarez is a jack-of-all-trades.

In his thirty-plus years on this planet, Juarez said, in many ways, he has witnessed the worst this world has to offer. Let's face it, farm work can be brutal. He recounted seeing his friends work until their fingers bled or their knees were too stiff to walk. Many of his friends are sick on a regular basis, but the last thing on their mind is missing work for a doctor's appointment. And worse, he often hears how their children are sick, but his friends never have the time or the money to take them to the clinic, unless it's really bad.

Because besides being brutal, migrant farmwork is competitive. Any given day, there's always someone a bit younger ready to work a bit harder, or take a bit more risk, and take your place in line. Desperation runs deep among unskilled workers as they try to eke out a better life for themselves and their families. If you don't show up for work, there is almost always someone who steps in to take your place.

Many critics blame farmers for taking advantage of unskilled laborers, especially for not providing basic benefits, such as healthcare. But Juarez said he sees the bigger picture. From his perspective, farmers can't afford those things because the competition in agriculture is so fierce.

Additionally, most migrant farmworkers are constantly on the move, rotating from one farm to another in or around California or even to different states. On the East Coast, farmworkers go from Florida to New Jersey throughout the year, working wherever, for whomever, whenever the next crop is ready.

The idea of getting to know a doctor who could get to know him and help him take care of himself and his family long term isn't something he's ever considered. "Not going to happen." Juarez laughed.

Juarez is lucky though—he has the skills to pick up odd jobs that keep him from chasing the crops every season and has established something of a home base. And that area is served by a local mobile health program, which he and his family have been fortunate enough to use, although according to him, "It's not here nearly enough."

"This is not really a good way of life. There's a lot of fear," Juarez said. "I don't mean anybody is going to hurt you—that stuff was the old days and doesn't really happen anymore—but the farmers remind us, all the time, they could get somebody else to work faster. They talk about how they are under pressure to get everything picked fast or else they're going to lose money.

"The pressure to be there every day, sunup to sundown, and to work at a crazy pace the whole time is unreal. But it's like they say, 'or else.'"

Out of necessity, Juarez taught himself to fix cars, starting with his own. He has never had any training, but he's good enough to work part-time at a local garage. Over the nearly two decades since he was in high school, Juarez has done just about every blue-collar, day-labor job you can imagine, from fixing cars to mowing lawns to flipping burgers. Basically, he is willing to do anything to keep food on the table and a roof over his family's head.

Juarez has a positive attitude about all that but says there is one thing he fears more than anything else: having someone in his family get sick.

"*No bueno*," said Juarez, who splices Spanish and English together in a prototypical version of Spanglish. Juarez is fluent in both languages and alternates from one to the other with ease, usually with a touch of humor.

His "*no bueno*" was said with a happy smile. However, behind the mask of good cheer, I picked up a flash of terror as he briefly considered the possibility. This raw reality reflects how much fear of illness and injury hangs over Juarez and his family—and millions of other farmworkers in California, Texas, Florida, and other states.

To stay front of mind for the people who pay him, Juarez makes sure he's around all the time, often lingering after finishing a job an extra half hour or so to see if maybe they think of something else or have something for him tomorrow.

"When the other guys go home to eat and drink, I stay back," he said with a chuckle. "What's that saying, out of sight, out of mind? Not Jose. Jose is always there."

"I work sixty hours a week, and that's without counting travel time, which is around two hours each way," he said. "When am I supposed to go to the doctor? Even when we have a Saturday option for the doctor, I'm trying to work."

If you're thinking, *Oh, his wife, then,* you'll be disappointed. The Bronco is the family car, at work with Juarez, and his wife doesn't have a driver's license. Rideshare services exist in their town, and they use them when they must, but those are expensive and inconsistent. More than once, his wife has had rides cancelled, forcing her to miss appointments scheduled months before.

For Juarez, the mobile health program was not sent out by the local health department but by God himself. The team shows up at his children's schools, where the kids receive basic preventative care and the immunizations the state requires to keep them enrolled in school.

When I told Juarez other services are provided through these programs, too, such as dental care, maternal care, behavioral health and substance abuse care, and even mental health counseling, I saw his eyes grow wide as he considered what having access to these services might mean for his family, friends, and coworkers.

The dental care hits home because Juarez had one coworker who kept losing his teeth. His friend was in constant pain and rarely slept well. "He could never drink anything cold, even when it was hot, because the pain would just kill him," Juarez said. "It was lukewarm water, all the time."

Drugs and alcohol abuse are a constant presence for migrant workers. Some use substances to dull body pains from working day after day bent over in the heat, but the alcohol and drugs mask larger problems. Juarez described how plenty of workers went from drinking alcohol some days to drinking alcohol every day and then to drinking alcohol all day.

When we talked about sexually transmitted diseases in the migrant communities, Juarez shook his head in disappointment. There is a lack of education and a lack of treatment options. Teen pregnancies and a lack of consistent maternal care are problematic. Simple things, such as birth control and condoms, are misunderstood.

For example, Juarez hears all sorts of odd ideas about when and how a woman can get pregnant and what to do when there's a new baby on the way. "People just say, 'We'll be fine,' or they think they can't get pregnant a certain way. You try to tell them, 'No, that's not how it works, amigo, but they don't want to hear it. Then, suddenly, a kid is on the way. I can't point fingers, because me and my wife were like that. A lot of these guys get a girl pregnant and then disappear. Or they go see [a sex worker] in town and they catch something. You hear about four or five guys getting the same thing because they all went to the same place." It is, to use Juarez's words, "a mess."

Juarez said most of the people he knows just need to know more about their health. They don't understand blood pressure, diabetes, or dental care. They don't understand how small problems can become big ones, like how not brushing your teeth leads to root canals.

They see doctors as part of the government, in some ways, especially when it comes to healthcare providers. For that reason, undocumented migrant farmworkers have an overwhelming fear that each time they're forced by their humanness to go to the doctor's office, they risk being discovered, arrested, and deported.

But when the doctors come to them on their turf, for most of them, that fear fades.

Juarez has seen both sides: how having access to healthcare can help and how losing access can hurt. "My wife had a job for a few years with insurance that covered our whole family," Juarez said. "But then she got laid off, so that hurt. It wasn't easy, even with insurance. It cost us a lot."

The conversation kept turning back to convenience and other priorities. "Man, really, the time is the thing. You want to take the kids to the doctor or even go yourself, but when? I'm somewhere working and she's somewhere working, and that's if we're lucky. When is there time?"

What about family? Friends? While the Juarez family has some extended family in the nearby communities of Los Banos and Modesto, nothing is a short drive here.

"Her parents went back to Mexico to take care of the grandparents. My parents are split up. Yeah, everybody tries to help everybody, but it's hard, you know, to ask and ask. If you ask somebody to watch your kids while you go to the doctor for yourself or with one of your other kids, you feel like you have to do the same thing for them," Juarez said. "It's like, 'Hey, you owe me a favor, what's up with you saying no?' People can get upset."

When his oldest son injured his leg playing soccer, the trips to the hospital and then for follow-up care were brutal. "The emergency room cost us more than $500 even after we begged and pleaded," said Juarez.

After that, they went to two follow-up appointments, which cost them several hundred dollars more. Then, despite the doctor ordering a third appointment, their son appeared to be fine, so they skipped it. Juarez said he felt guilty not taking his son to the last appointment.

"What are you supposed to do, tell your kid to not go play? All us parents talk about the same thing: 'Don't let your kids play on the phone or computer all day.' Our kids don't have phones, and they go to friends if they want to play on a computer or something like that, but it's all the same. You want them to be outside, run around, be healthy, all the stuff we did as kids," he said.

"But I'd be lying if I told you I don't worry about him or his sisters getting hurt again and having to go to the hospital. Worse, what happens when we can't go? Everybody says, 'It's only money,' but then you gotta deal with the pressure about how you're going to pay and what bills you have to put off," he said.

On more than one occasion, Juarez and his family have had the electricity in their house turned off for several days as they literally had to pick and choose what they could pay for.

In that world, regular medical care is an absolute luxury that features numerous considerations. Yearly checkups and testing for hypertension, prediabetes, or kidney disease are not just simple to-dos; they are luxuries.

That worries Juarez, not only for himself, but for his family. Several of his distant family members suffered with heart issues. He doesn't know if those issues were isolated to those individual family members or are something that will impact him one day. He pushes his body to extremes on a regular basis, and despite being in his thirties, he already has persistent neck and back problems. He also experiences a fair amount of swelling and inflammation in his feet and knees.

He said he tries not to think about the pain because it goes away when he has a day off. Still, when he plays with his children or handles the handyman list at the little apartment he and his wife rent, the pain doesn't go away as quickly as it used to.

Looking at the lines on his face, the calloused hands, and the reddish-brown tint on his cheeks, Juarez looks a lot closer to fifty than thirty. While he's a happy person, there is no question that he's lived a life much tougher than mine.

He doesn't care much about how he looks, but he did bring up that his wife and children are easily annoyed when they get stares. "I know it's kind of stupid, but you get tired of people looking down at you because your shoes or clothes are a little dirty or old."

And at the hospital, he thinks everyone is suspicious they are undocumented and are somehow milking the system. Most of the time, that doesn't come up, simply because there are so many people of Mexican or Latin descent living in their area. But when it does, it is usually when getting some kind of medical treatment. Juarez said his daughters usually feel uncomfortable about going to the doctor. However, when they went to a mobile clinic, the discomfort disappeared.

"That was actually fun for them," Juarez said. "They were thinking this was like a ride, like at the county fair. The nurses showed them up front, and they let them sit in the driver's seat. So did my son. I just wish they could do it more often or maybe come to the schools every week. We need a lot more of this here."

Jose Juarez represents one hundred million Americans who aren't asking for much. They don't want free healthcare or government handouts. They want dignity. They want their kids to sit in the driver's seat and not feel ashamed of their dirty shoes. They want to be seen as human beings, not problems to be solved.

The question isn't whether we can afford to bring healthcare to people like Jose. The question is whether we can afford not to.

Chapter 7
“We Force Them to Follow Our Rules”

Dr. Daniella Jaimes-Colina discovered the power of mobile healthcare not in a conference room or a research study but in the mountains of Venezuela, where showing up meant the difference between life and death.

For eight years, she practiced medicine from the passenger seat of a jeep, bouncing over dirt paths that barely qualified as roads to reach patients in remote villages. Sometimes she’d conduct examinations right there in the jeep. Sometimes in a classroom at the local school. Sometimes in patients’ homes. If someone was seriously ill, she’d load them into the jeep and drive them back to a hospital, bouncing through mountain passes with precious cargo.

“Literally, we would have to use the jeeps because these weren’t always exactly roads, you know, to get to these little towns,” she said, half-joking and half-incredulous at the memory. “It was rough to get up there.”

When Dr. Jaimes-Colina arrived in Florida in 2013, she called her friends back in Venezuela to describe the resources she now had at her disposal. "It was like being in Disney World," she told them. After years of practicing with expired medications and makeshift examination rooms, America felt like a medical wonderland.

Yet for all those resources, she discovered something troubling: The very abundance of American healthcare had created distance between providers and patients.

"When a patient comes to us, we force them to follow our rules, our process, our strict workflows," Dr. Jaimes-Colina explained. "The system sets the tone and time and intensity."

Everyone knows the routine. You carry your stress and anxiety to the check-in counter. If your insurance is in order, you take a seat and wait. Finally, someone calls your name, and you're swept into the inner sanctum to be processed through a series of stations: vitals, blood draw, nurse's questions, more waiting. Then the doctor appears for a few minutes to deliver their verdict before moving on to the next patient.

Despite the good intentions of healthcare workers, the system often feels impersonal and rushed. For many patients, especially those from underserved communities, a trip to the doctor's office can feel intimidating, even foreboding.

Dr. Jaimes-Colina saw this firsthand when she began working in Central Florida. In the Pine Hills section of Orlando, just west of downtown, she found a community that had been largely abandoned by traditional healthcare despite having safety-net clinics, such as federally qualified health centers, nearby.

Pine Hills had once been a thriving middle-class neighborhood built in the 1950s for Lockheed Martin employees. It even had its own country club. But decades of neglect had transformed it into an area plagued by poverty and crime. The country club became an apartment building. The community became known as Crime Hills.

Even though healthcare facilities existed in the area, the community wasn't engaging. Health outcomes were terrible. Hypertension and diabetes were rampant.

Then COVID-19 hit.

Orange County bought a trailer to test and vaccinate people who were sheltering in place during the pandemic. Dr. Jaimes-Colina and her team took it to Pine Hills, among other places.

The trailer was uncomfortable—no insulation meant it was freezing in the mornings and blazing hot in the afternoons. But as Dr. Jaimes-Colina said, with the spirit of mobile health champions everywhere, "We made it work!" At the height of the pandemic, her team was administering four thousand COVID-19 tests a day.

More importantly, something unprecedented was happening. For the first time, Pine Hills residents were receiving healthcare services in their own community. Trust began to build. The program expanded.

"When we go to them, in many ways now we follow their rules—we have to fit in their community, their culture," Dr. Jaimes-Colina explained. "This movement toward them is humanizing the system. We are in their environment, we can see their social determinants of health, we breathe the same air, see their transportation with our own eyes. It's like a veil falls between the patient and the provider, and it's impossible for you, as a medical provider, not to understand their reality and their circumstances."

The team launched a Know Your Numbers campaign, teaching patients about blood pressure, blood sugar, and other vital health metrics. They rewrapped the van with the slogan so the message would sink in. Patients who had been reluctant to share any personal information suddenly wanted to get tested and learn what their numbers meant.

"We're talking about people who didn't trust the system and were very wary about giving up any type of information about themselves,"

Dr. Jaimes-Colina said. "Suddenly, here they are asking to get tested and eager to learn what their numbers actually mean."

Building trust required meeting people where they were—literally. "If we sent a nurse out to give information, she would go to the barber shop or the car wash to find the men she wanted to see. That's what you have to do in those neighborhoods to take care of people."

The impact was profound. Showing up—making the effort to be present in someone's neighborhood—sends a powerful message to the community about caring. When a person sees a healthcare provider willing to drive to their community, it says, "You're important to me. I care about you. Don't give up on yourself. You're not alone."

"For the patient, it's impossible to unsee that," Dr. Jaimes-Colina said. "They can't unsee the chance to have access to healthcare. Everybody sees that van, and they can touch it. There is no wall up around the mobile unit; there is no big building that they have to drive around to find a parking spot. There's no waiting room."

The results spoke for themselves. When data was compared to similar communities with better healthcare access, Pine Hills showed dramatic improvements in controlled hypertension and diabetes measures. The Know Your Numbers project reached its goal of serving 2,500 patients in less than two years. Today, the program is known as the Community Outreach Awareness Community Health mobile medical office, continuing to serve at-risk residents throughout Orange County.

But even after years in the US, Dr. Jaimes-Colina says the most powerful example of mobile health's impact came from a patient in Venezuela.

One of her patients was a fourteen-year-old girl in a small mountain town who was pregnant and dealing with all the associated risks. The girl's diet was poor, mostly carbohydrates, and she was developing hypertension. Every time Dr. Jaimes-Colina visited that town, she made sure to sit with the girl.

"I kept telling her that just because she has a child now is not the end of her developing and building her own life," she said. "I wanted her to know that to support her baby, she had to go back to school and finish her education and have a successful life."

Over the next five months, Dr. Jaimes-Colina and other healthcare workers helped the young girl understand nutrition and get better food. They taught her about birthing options. They even gave her a baby shower, turning what could have been a desperate situation into something positive.

"This was a situation where you could see right from the start that if we didn't help, she was going to have issues, and the birth was probably going to end up being an emergency C-section," she said. "But because we had earned the trust of the people in her community and eventually with her, we were able to help, and she was able to have a beautiful, healthy baby."

As Dr. Jaimes-Colina told this story, excitement and joy poured through her voice. This captures what so many healthcare workers feel about mobile health—it allows them to impact the lives of people at greatest risk, which is why they got into healthcare in the first place.

Critics often worry about the costs and complexity of mobile healthcare. Dr. Jaimes-Colina has a simple response: "Complexity is the enemy. Every time we add a layer of complexity into caring about people, we are restricting access, and our problems get worse. If we keep access to care at the center of the strategy, many public health challenges resolve themselves."

She's equally direct about the business model: "Everyone worries about the business side instead of focusing on the fact that better access drives better outcomes. I always have the public health perspective, so I don't see this in terms of cost. Look at it from a perspective of population health—you can clearly see the data for populations that have access to healthcare versus populations that do not."

The real power of mobile health isn't in a van or dental equipment, she insists. "It is the people … It's having a nurse who can go to a barber shop and talk to people about who we are, whom we're here for, and what we are here to share that might help them."

Mobile health fundamentally changes the relationship between provider and patient. Instead of processing people through a system, it creates space for genuine human connection.

"No matter how different we are, we have one thing in common: No one likes to be sick," Dr. Jaimes-Colina said. "In mobile health, you can normalize a health conversation, not just process people through the system. We want to make sure people aren't sick, and if they are sick, they get better. And being in their space allows you to work with them, not on them, and walk with them on their journey, side by side, as a person, not just a provider."

My friend John taught me something that captures the essence of what Dr. Jaimes-Colina learned in those mountains of Venezuela: "You can't lead people until you find them." That's not just good medicine. That's good leadership.

Chapter 8

"Compassion Is Not Just a Spoken Word"

Dr. Salvador Sandoval is seventy-four years old and has spent more than fifty years in medicine, primarily caring for those in the greatest need.

He has the drawing to prove it.

Sitting in Dr. Sandoval's home is a framed portrait of him done by Kevin Baugh, a patient and homeless man who had incredible artistic talent. Baugh, who died of cancer several years ago, was so talented that people would buy the signs he drew to beg for money and food.

"He had this one that he drew one time of a hamburger with an arrow pointing down to a heart and someone literally paid him for the drawing, and he had to make another sign," Dr. Sandoval said. "That would happen all the time."

The drawing shows the two of them together, with Dr. Sandoval standing above a seated Baugh as they shake hands. Sandoval looks like a classic doctor you might see in a 1950s television show. The image resonates with warmth, friendliness, and trust. It's also inscribed with a message in Baugh's beautiful handwriting: "Compassion is best expressed by what is in one's heart. We are blessed that for Dr. Sandoval compassion is not just a spoken word. Dr. Sandoval & his staff's dedication to those less fortunate are greatly appreciated and we thank you."

Dr. Sandoval and Baugh met in the late 1990s when Sandoval was working on a mobile health program run by Golden Valley Healthcare (GVHC) in the northern part of California's vast Central Valley. GVHC had started the program to help care for homeless patients, and Sandoval was part of a rotation of doctors who would go out every Tuesday to serve a homeless shelter in Merced.

The community had quickly learned the schedule of this new source of help and hospitality. Although Baugh didn't use the shelter, he was one of several homeless people who would show up regularly for care. Through those visits, Baugh learned he could trust Dr. Sandoval.

Baugh was many things during his life. He was an artist who, while troubled by drug addiction, was still loved dearly by his family. He was also fiercely independent and prideful despite his condition. Whenever city officials tried to get him to move out of the shack he had built under a freeway, he would protest and tell them this was his place in the world and where he felt he could best protect his artwork and belongings.

To an observer, Baugh's logic seemed twisted by his own perceptions and distrust of the system. But the depth of that departure from "normal thinking" serves as emblematic of the trust gap Dr. Sandoval was able to bridge with Baugh and others experiencing the same challenges.

Dr. Sandoval's ability to connect with patients like Baugh didn't happen by accident. It was forged through decades of experience treating people others had given up on.

Dr. Sandoval graduated from the University of California at San Diego Medical School in 1975 and then interned at Los Angeles County Hospital shortly afterward. Located at the intersection of Interstate 5 and Interstate 10 in downtown Los Angeles, Los Angeles County Hospital was a bubbling cauldron of activity. From shootings to stabbings to car accidents to deliveries of children, Dr. Sandoval saw it all.

"It was amazing training," said Dr. Sandoval, who trained to be a family physician and even delivered one hundred babies in one month during his time at Los Angeles County. "You would see anything and everything coming through there, and it gave you this amazing experience in how to treat everyone. I didn't stay because I eventually would have had to end up as an ER/trauma doctor, but I got a chance to experience so much and deal with so many different types of people."

Critically, that experience offered the opportunity to treat patients with what is commonly referred to as adverse childhood experiences (ACEs), so he understood at a visceral level the reactions and manifestations that came with those experiences. ACEs are potentially traumatic events—such as abuse, neglect, or household dysfunction, including parental substance abuse or incarceration—that occur before age eighteen and are linked to increased risk of chronic disease, mental illness, and reduced life expectancy in adulthood.[25] He learned not to judge people by their circumstances but to see the person beneath the pain.

He put that experience and understanding to use when he came to Merced. Working with people suffering from substance abuse disorder, he would often encounter children from homes broken because of drugs

25 "About Adverse Childhood Experiences," Centers for Disease Control and Prevention, September 24, 2025, https://www.cdc.gov/aces/about/index.html.

or domestic violence. There were mothers and fathers who desperately wanted to get clean. And others were just trying to survive.

Dr. Sandoval's path to mobile health began in the 1990s when then Governor Pete Wilson declared a state of emergency responding to a cold-weather crisis. With overnight temperatures in the area dipping into the twenties, Wilson opened National Guard armories that dot the area to help house the homeless population and avoid deaths from exposure.

Dr. Sandoval was then working for and was on the board of the Golden Valley Health Centers, which now serves the San Joaquin Valley with more than fifty locations. He contributed to Governor Wilson's effort to protect the homeless by moving supplies and medicine to the armories.

The episode of caring for the homeless on location outside office hours inspired him to step up to lead GVHC's mobile health program years later and expand it to serve the local agricultural workers.

"The farmers love what we do for a couple of reasons," Dr. Sandoval said. "First, they know they can't afford to provide healthcare coverage for their workers, so this fills that gap. Second, they know they can't afford for people to miss work. When we're able to come to them and help keep the farmworkers healthy, it doesn't take them away from their jobs."

The work at the homeless shelter was particularly gratifying because he could see the growth in trust by the patients. Like every program, trust might seem slow to build, but he saw consistent progress. People in need of help—with diabetes, high blood pressure, and COPD treatments, all conditions that impact homeless people at a much higher rate than the normal population—started to come around. It was working.

And as word spread, trust extended to an even more at-risk patient group: drug addicts.

"Word got around quick that people could come see me and I could be trusted to help them, even for heroin users," Dr. Sandoval said. "I went into those conversations just valuing them as people and giving them the respect they deserve. We knew exactly how to help, physically, but trust was the real key to helping them."

Baugh, who was a methamphetamine user for parts of his life, was a testimony to that trust.

"The biggest thing was not to judge people. Baugh was a great example," Dr. Sandoval said. "There was a point where he was not using drugs but claiming that he was. I knew he was clean because his tests would come back clean. The first time he did it, I let it go and didn't say anything. The next time, I told him that I knew he wasn't being truthful, but it was OK. I wasn't judging him; I just wanted to know what was going on and make sure he was OK. That's when he was honest with me and said he was turning around and selling the drugs. After that, we were able to address the real need."

From Dr. Sandoval's perspective, treating substance abuse disorders is one of the most effective use cases for mobile health programs in the area he serves. The ability to reach so many people with drugs such as SUBOXONE, which helps decrease the withdrawal symptoms that come with drug use, is key.

"You have so many people trying to turn their lives around, but it's so hard for them. So many times, they have alienated just about everyone around them. They have stolen from friends and family until those people finally can't take it anymore. They have humiliated themselves in their own mind and feel worthless and/or hopeless. That is such a hard cycle to break out of because it becomes as much mental as physical," Dr. Sandoval said.

The advantage to mobile health programs in this regard is that it isn't around the "normal" healthcare but a bit off the grid. There is no waiting in a doctor's office with other people around, staring at you. For those battling drug addiction, there is often a heightened sense of paranoia that feeds the whirlwind of long-entrenched embarrassment and shame. The sheer idea that people are staring at them and their demons is too much. Humans avoid what makes us feel bad.

A mobile health clinic is a far less intimidating environment. There is usually one patient at a time, safely closed off a bit from the world but only a few steps from the street, their belongings, and total freedom. The care sites are established in areas where patients feel at home and comfortable.

While a homeless shelter might not sound like a comfortable environment to many people, it is—no matter how strange that seems—what many people call home. It is familiar and free of judgment. For immigrants or addicts, there is less fear that the police or other government agencies will be lurking.

The mobile health programs in Dr. Sandoval's area have proven remarkably adaptable. Those organizations have flexibility to communicate and coordinate and shift what they are doing very quickly to meet the needs of the community. They can be in downtown Merced or travel to Los Banos, a farming community forty miles away, to help care for the many homeless people who live there. The need is acute and ongoing; some people struggle to get a hot shower on a regular basis. During the pandemic, the mobile health programs shifted to become immunization hubs.

But Dr. Sandoval has also seen what happens when mobile health programs aren't properly coordinated or sustained.

"What makes mobile health successful is a solid plan and a lot of effort in terms of community coordination," he said. "Here there are three different services in the area that provide mobile healthcare, which is wonderful."

Still, without coordination and commitment of the community, Dr. Sandoval says a good start can easily lose momentum.

"I've seen a lot of enthusiasm and interest in mobile health flare up over the years, and suddenly people and organizations are pouring money into it, but without a real plan about how to sustain it," he said. "The need is there, and mobile model's potential to fill the gap is great, but the planning required and the need to change over time depending on local variables can make it hard to remain focused if there is no system for managing."

When the priority three months ago isn't the priority today, and the organizations that run the mobile health programs don't have a system to manage that reprioritization and work together to adjust, there can be a very quick decline in the efficiency of what the mobile units are doing.

"When that happens, suddenly, these organizations are not getting the return on investment that they expected to be getting. When it turns out this is hard work versus simply stroking a check, interest and excitement wane very fast. Trying to revive a program is twice as hard as starting one, because when it wasn't easy, people don't believe it works," Dr. Sandoval said.

To Dr. Sandoval, Baugh's artwork is more than an appreciation. It is a representation of why he got into helping others in the first place. He sees his patients as people with stories and talents who have fallen on hard times but can be saved. Baugh was a man of great talent and pride who found, in Dr. Sandoval, someone who saw his humanity before his homelessness, his art before his addiction.

That drawing hangs in Dr. Sandoval's home as a reminder of what's possible when healthcare providers meet patients where they are, without judgment, with only the intention to help. It's a testament to the power of trust—the real key to working wonders in the Golden Valley and everywhere else mobile health takes root.

Chapter 9

The Smile That Changed Everything

Dr. Jesse Schwartz turned away from his patient so the boy wouldn't see him cry.

Dr. Schwartz was in the Dominican Republic finishing his dental school requirements with a community health rotation. The rules were simple: one procedure per patient, maybe a filling or extraction, then move on. There were too many people in need and not enough time.

But this child's teeth were a disaster—gnarled from abnormal growth and years of poor hygiene. Kids at school made fun of him. He covered his mouth when he spoke. He had learned not to smile.

When the shy boy sat down in his chair, Dr. Schwartz couldn't follow the rules.

"We had these rules, but if there ever was a time to be a rule breaker, this was it. We gathered everything we could, extra bonding material, whatever we could find, and we went to work," said Dr. Schwartz, who now specializes in cosmetic dentistry but still remembers that moment as the one that changed everything.

When they finished, the boy stared at himself in the mirror. His face transformed. For the first time in years, maybe ever, he smiled—a real smile, wide and unashamed.

"I could feel how happy he was," Dr. Schwartz said. "No one was able to make fun of him anymore. He wasn't going to be embarrassed or humiliated. Besides the clean teeth, he just had a different look on his face."

That's when Dr. Schwartz had to turn away. In a pure moment of empathy and accomplishment, he wept. He had just witnessed something profound: A smile doesn't just reflect good feelings—it creates them.

The boy in the Dominican Republic taught Dr. Schwartz something that would shape his entire career. Your mouth isn't separate from the rest of your body or your emotional well-being. It's all connected. When you fix someone's teeth, you're fixing far more than teeth.

Dr. Jeri Andrews learned this lesson, too, but in a very different setting. As chief medical officer for CareSouth Carolina, she's seen things that still shock her after years in rural healthcare.

"The first time you see this with your own eyes, it kind of boggles your mind," Dr. Andrews said. "You think, this can't be real. We're in the United States!"

What she's talking about are teenagers—eighteen-year-olds getting full sets of dentures after years of poor education and hygiene. In some counties she serves, there are zero dentists. Zero. Kids grow up never seeing one, never learning to brush properly, never understanding that tooth pain isn't just something you live with.

"There's just so much you want to help people understand about how important it is just to take basic care of your teeth," Dr. Andrews said. "Believe it or not, brushing is a foreign concept to a lot of people. The people we're seeing just don't have the money for toothpaste or a toothbrush, much less a visit to a dentist."

She's arrived at schools with basic brushing kits—the kind most people get every six months at the dentist—and had to explain to kids what they are, what they do, and how to use them.

The tragedy isn't only cosmetic. Research shows the connection between oral health and overall health is substantial—strong enough that doctors should treat your mouth as a window into your entire body's condition. Bad gums often signal diabetes, heart disease, or other chronic conditions. Tooth pain leads to emergency room visits that cost thousands of dollars for problems that could have been prevented with basic care.

But in rural South Carolina, like in many parts of America, the barriers are overwhelming.

"What you see in these places are time and transportation problems," Dr. Andrews said. "A patient's inability to get time off work to go to the doctor or take their children to the doctor. Even if they have time, a lot of people don't have a car or even access to someone else's car. Even if they had a car, or a ride, they don't have money for gas."

So, children grow up with mouths full of pain, learning to cover their smiles, just like the boy in the Dominican Republic. Except this is happening in America, where we know how to prevent it.

Dr. Jordan Combs saw the same problems in California's Central Valley. As a fourth-generation resident whose family were farmers, he grew up understanding the struggles of agricultural workers who make America's food but can't afford basic healthcare.

When he toured a mobile dental clinic for the first time, his head was spinning with possibilities.

Dr. Combs is built like a football player—big, gregarious, with thick arms that serve him well during tough tooth extractions. He's the kind of dentist who drives to San Francisco at three in the morning to spend the day fishing in the Bay, then comes back ready to do it again the next weekend.

He's also one of the few dentists working in Golden Valley Health Centers' mobile health program, bringing dental care directly to farmworkers who can't leave their jobs or afford to miss a day's pay.

His family were farmers at first, so it bothers him when he sees farmworkers struggle to get adequate healthcare, he told us. He moves comfortably among his largely Mexican American patients, many of whom speak primarily Spanish and have come to trust him as both a guide and protector.

Dr. Combs could be making more money in private practice, but he's searching for significance beyond success. The mobile dental program gives him something no traditional practice could: the ability to go exactly where he's needed most.

"There's obviously a tension to resolve getting people who go through dental school or medical school to understand that community health can also work out financially for them," Dr. Combs said. "You've just spent a lot of money to go to school, and now you have to pay it back. It's hard to see early on how the best path might not be private practice."

But the rewards can't be overstated. Instead of waiting and worrying about patients who can't get to him, Dr. Combs makes the first move. He shrinks the distance between himself and his patients. He goes to their schools, their community centers, their workplaces.

From South Carolina to California, from the Dominican Republic to rural America, the story is the same: People are living with pain and shame that could be prevented. Children are learning not to smile. Teenagers are getting dentures. Adults are avoiding social situations because they're embarrassed about their teeth.

But mobile health is changing that equation. When dental care comes to the patient instead of the other way around, barriers disappear. Transportation isn't an issue. Missing work isn't a problem. The care meets people where they are, both literally and figuratively.

When mobile dental programs roll into underserved communities, they're not just preventing cavities. They're preventing emergency room visits, chronic diseases, and a lifetime of covering your mouth when you speak. They're giving people back their smiles—and everything that comes with them.

That boy in the Dominican Republic taught Dr. Schwartz something that every mobile health provider learns: When you help someone smile again, you're changing their whole world. And sometimes, if you're paying attention, it changes yours too.

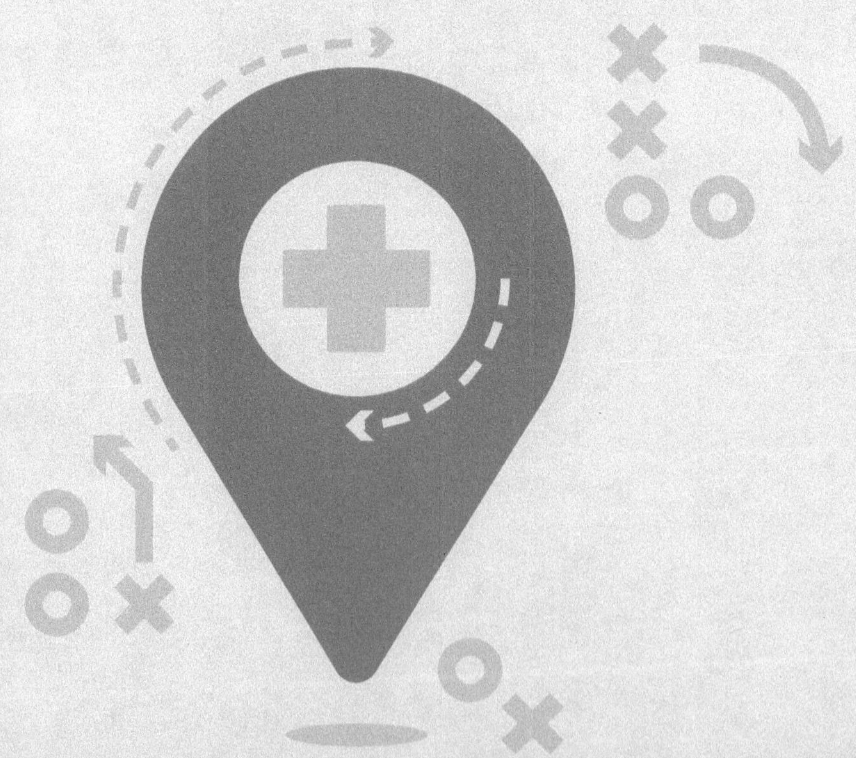

Chapter 10

From Chicago to Thailand—the View from Thirty Thousand Feet

Six-year-old Niran had never seen so many people in his village.

The dusty streets of his rural Thai community were suddenly alive with color—red tents sprouting like flowers, volunteers in bright yellow shirts directing traffic, children running between booths with balloons tied to their wrists. The smell of street food mixed with the antiseptic scent of medical equipment being unpacked from trucks.

Ronald McDonald House Charities' (RMHC) annual mobile health festival had kicked off, and for Niran, this was about to become the most important day of his young life.

His grandmother, who had raised him since his parents died in a motorcycle accident, held his hand tightly as they approached the dental tent. Niran's mouth had been hurting for months, but the nearest dentist was a three-hour bus ride away—a journey they couldn't afford.

"It's OK, little one," his grandmother whispered in Thai. "These people came all this way just to help you."

What she didn't know was that this single day would spark a chain reaction that would transform not just Niran's life but the entire way their community thought about healthcare.

Half a world away, in the Chicago offices of RMHC, Hye Kim was tracking the impact of festivals just like this one. As director of research program evaluation and advocacy, she'd been with RMHC since 2016, but she could still remember the first time she witnessed what happened when mobile healthcare became community celebration.

"There's a remarkable level of energy in these events," Kim said, her voice lighting up as she recalled visiting the Thailand program. "It's the same in Indonesia, where they do vaccinations and immunizations. They have a similar health education fair, and the entire community shows up. It's really a magical public health moment."

Kim understood something that many healthcare organizations miss: The most powerful thing you can do isn't just to provide medical care but to build trust. And trust, she'd learned, spreads like wildfire when entire communities rally around protecting their children.

The numbers told the story: forty mobile health programs worldwide, operating in Asia, Europe, and the United States. But Kim knew the real impact couldn't be measured in statistics alone.

Back in Thailand, Niran's dental examination revealed what his grandmother had feared—severe decay that would require multiple visits to fix properly. But here's what made this day different: It wasn't just about the dentistry.

The RMHC team had spent months coordinating with local government and armed forces to turn their mobile health visit into something unprecedented. As dentists from nearby towns volunteered their time, other providers offered physical exams, testing, and immunizations. Barbers gave free haircuts. Community health workers moved through the crowd, explaining in local dialects why vaccines were important, why dental care mattered, why taking care of yourself wasn't selfish but essential.

It was healthcare as community festival, prevention as celebration.

"We've found the most powerful thing we can do is to bring community health workers," Kim explained. "Their talents and training are in talking to people, educating them, and helping them understand why something like a vaccine, while maybe scary, is so important for their child. It has been remarkable to see them come into a community, engage people in these conversations, and see communities come together to protect their children."

The Thai Red Cross was there in full force, managing crowds and providing support. Local leaders got their vaccinations publicly, sending the message that if it was good enough for them, it was good enough for everyone. Children watched their parents and community leaders engage with the healthcare providers, reinforcing the cultural concept that health mattered to the group.

For Niran, the festival was only the beginning. The dental work would take several visits, but the RMHC team had already coordinated his follow-up care with local providers. His grandmother had been educated about oral hygiene and given supplies to help maintain Niran's dental health at home.

But the real transformation happened in the weeks that followed. Word spread through the village about the care people had received. Parents who had been hesitant about vaccines brought their children to the local health post. People began talking openly about health problems they'd been hiding. The festival hadn't just provided healthcare—it had changed how the community thought about healthcare.

"If you do that year after year, it sends a clear message that if we're there, people should show up," Kim said. "Basically, if we're there, this is something that can be trusted. You say to people, 'Please come,' and they do without hesitation."

This is what made RMHC's global mobile health program different. It wasn't just about bringing medical care to remote areas—it was about building lasting relationships, changing cultural attitudes, and creating sustainable systems of care.

The model worked because of meticulous preparation. Months before each festival, staff contacted parents and caregivers, coordinated care plans, and ensured all paperwork was completed. Each child had forms filled and signed long before the first dental professional set foot on-site. The Thai Red Cross was prepared to manage crowds and provide support.

But the real secret was understanding that healthcare happens in the context of communities. In Latvia, where RMHC runs similar programs, they discovered that reaching entire populations lacking healthcare access required more than just showing up with medical equipment. It required becoming part of the community's social fabric. And that required Kim and her team to think differently about sustainability.

"You are typically talking about a large capital investment in equipment," Kim acknowledged. "The mobile clinics we use have always been very expensive. They need medical equipment on board. All that must be maintained for years, so we consider life cycle costs."

These financial challenges were real, and donor funding was expected to deliver measurable results. Operational costs are often harder to fundraise for than flashy new equipment, and it is difficult to track long-term outcomes in communities when people move frequently or programs lack consistent contact information.

But the festivals, to Kim, weren't just healthcare delivery—they were community investment, relationship building, and cultural change.

Six months after the festival, Niran's dental work was complete. His grandmother noticed he smiled more, spoke more clearly, and seemed more confident at school. But the changes went deeper than that.

The village now had a relationship with healthcare providers. People understood prevention was possible, that pain didn't have to be endured, that taking care of yourself was important. When the next RMHC festival was announced, people didn't only show up—they even helped organize it.

"Yes, it's tough to get consistent data month to month, or year to year," Kim admitted. "You may have a child, we'll call him Johnny, and Johnny shows up out of nowhere and sees a dentist for the first time ever. So, now you're trying to keep up with this child, because you want to see him again in six months. Six months goes by, and you don't see him. Why? Who knows."

But one thing Kim has learned is that the most important changes can't be measured in traditional ways. When a grandmother discovered that healthcare wasn't something that happened to you but something you could participate in, when a community realized that taking care of each other was both possible and powerful—those are the outcomes that matter most.

RMHC had discovered something profound: The most sustainable mobile health programs weren't just about bringing healthcare to people. They were about bringing people together around healthcare, creating communities where taking care of yourself and your neighbors becomes not just possible but celebrated.

For Niran, the festival that changed everything wasn't just about fixing his teeth. It was about discovering that he lived in a community that cared enough to make sure he could smile without pain, learn without distraction, and grow up knowing that his health mattered.

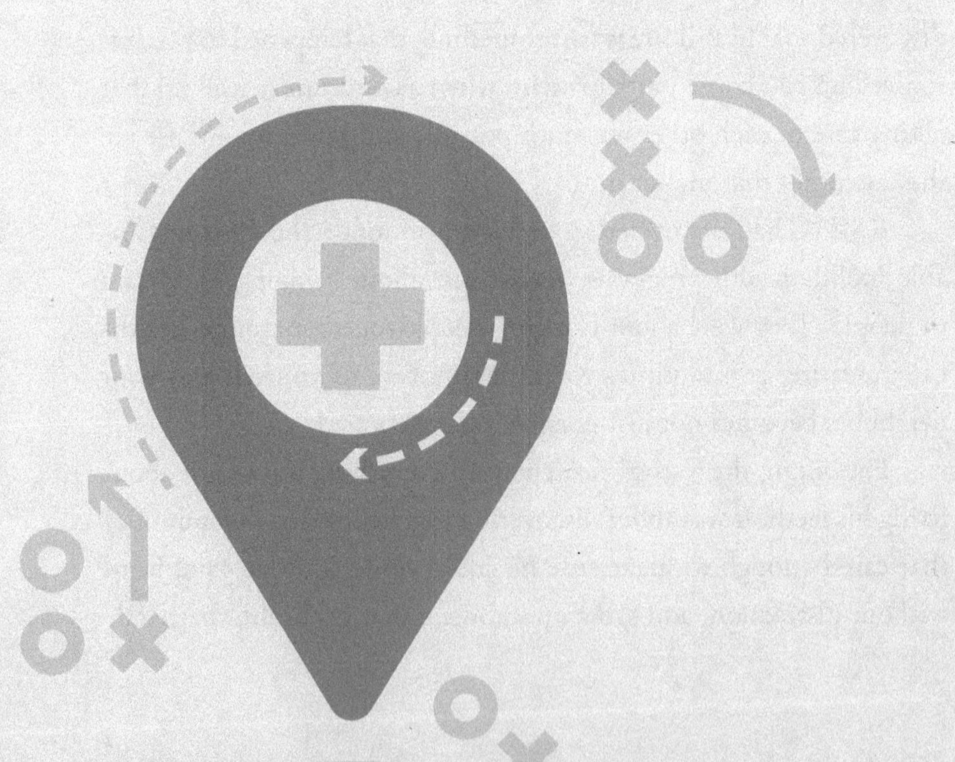

Chapter 11
One ER Doc's Revelation

Dr. Phil Levy had to step away from the family for a minute.

He'd just told them that their father—a man who should have had decades left to live—had died from a stroke. A stroke that could have been entirely prevented with better blood pressure control, better awareness, better access to basic preventive care.

Dr. Levy, an emergency medicine professor at Wayne State University in Detroit, had witnessed that scene too many times. A forty-five-year-old with end-stage heart failure. A mother of three whose diabetes had spiraled out of control. People dying from diseases that didn't have to kill them.

"I've had to tell the family of a fifty-year-old that their loved one just died from a stroke when it could have been entirely prevented," Dr. Levy said, his voice carrying the weight of those conversations. "We know which things save more lives than anything else—blood pressure medication, cholesterol medication, and smoking cessation. But until we start to own this problem of how we're going to do preventative care at scale, this country will continue to have people suffer unnecessarily from complications of a failed system."

Dr. Levy talks fast, thinks fast, reacts quickly—skills that serve him well in the high-pressure environment of emergency medicine. But speed couldn't solve the fundamental problem he saw every day: people showing up in crisis with conditions that should have been caught and treated years earlier.

Then the COVID-19 pandemic shattered Dr. Levy's assumptions about what was possible.

"During COVID, people had to get their own test, take it, and figure out what to do with the result. They had to figure out if they wanted a vaccine and where they were going to get it. They did it quite successfully. People figured it out," Dr. Levy said.

For someone who'd spent years watching the healthcare system fail his patients, this was a revelation. If people could navigate COVID-19 testing and vaccination—often through drive-through centers and mobile clinics—why couldn't they do the same with hypertension, diabetes, and other chronic conditions?

Working with Wayne State, Dr. Levy created Michigan's first drive-through COVID-19 testing facilities. In the early days, only first responders and healthcare workers could use the sites because of limited supplies. But as testing expanded and Ford Motor Company loaned vehicles to help take services into communities, Dr. Levy realized that the traditional model of healthcare delivery was broken, but mobile health could fix it.

"Quickly thereafter, we realized we needed to get into communities and use this geospatial analysis to target deployment," Dr. Levy said. "Michigan being Michigan, I reached out to the Ford company, which was very happy to loan me vehicles and grant advance money to start taking services directed by data into communities."

What started as COVID-19 response became a blueprint for preventing the tragedies he'd witnessed in the ER.

Dr. Levy's research portfolio tells the story of America's health crisis. As an associate vice president for translational science and fellow in multiple professional societies, he's overseen more than 110 studies over the past twenty years.[26] The data is consistent and heartbreaking: In his experience, approximately 85 percent of ER patients who come in with hypertension-related problems get discharged within twenty-four to forty-eight hours.

They're not sick enough to stay in the hospital, but they're not well enough to stay out of it either. They're caught in the gap between crisis and prevention—exactly where mobile health could make the biggest difference.

Here's the statistic that haunts him: Only 20 percent of Americans have their blood pressure under control.[27] If that number reached 80 percent, heart attacks and strokes would drop by 25 to 50 percent.[28] That's not a small improvement; that's a transformation that could save hundreds of thousands of lives.

"If we could get them in preventive care instead of showing up in the ER, just make sure they don't end up there, we'd solve way more problems than any amount of research," Dr. Levy said.

"That's a big, fishable pond, when you think about it," he added. "There are many parts of a program to get right, but the bottom line is that we need to meet people where they are."

The COVID-19 experience taught Dr. Levy something else: Patients were more capable than the healthcare system gave them

---

26 "Phillip D Levy (ap0229)," Wayne State University, accessed December 25, 2025, https://wayne.edu/people/ap0229.

27 Yechiam Ostchega et al., "Hypertension Prevalence, Awareness, Treatment, and Control Among Adults: United States, August 2021–August 2023," *NCHS Data Brief*, no. 511 (2024): CS354233.

28 Dena Ettehad et al., "Blood Pressure Lowering for Prevention of Cardiovascular Disease and Death: A Systematic Review and Meta-Analysis," *The Lancet* 387, no. 10022 (2016): 957–67, https://doi.org/10.1016/S0140-6736(15)01225-8.

credit for. When forced to take charge of their own health during the pandemic, people rose to the challenge. They figured out testing, vaccination, and self-management in ways that surprised even experienced healthcare providers.

"We've always hoped that could happen in healthcare," Dr. Levy said. "We have a moment in time that comes out of the pandemic where you have an engaged population which is becoming aware that they are going to have to take charge of their own healthcare."

This patient empowerment, combined with mobile health technology, created an unprecedented opportunity. Dr. Levy began envisioning a world where preventive care wasn't something you had to travel to receive—it came to you, in your community, at your workplace, in your neighborhood.

"Making preventive service fully accessible for everyone is the paradigm shift that needs to occur," Dr. Levy said. "But we can't even get the basics right. We can't even get most people's blood pressure under control."

The solution wasn't more research or more hospitals. It was taking basic preventive care directly to the people who needed it most.

With funding from the state, CARES Act dollars, and grants from the American Heart Association and National Institutes of Health, Dr. Levy began putting his vision into practice. Mobile clinics equipped with blood pressure monitors, lab equipment, and skilled nurses could reach underserved populations where they lived and worked.

The beauty of the model was its simplicity and efficiency. Almost all testing for chronic conditions could be done without a doctor present. Nurses and other clinicians could handle blood pressure checks, diabetes screenings, and health education—freeing up physicians to tackle procedures that truly required their expertise.

"The idea that a wellness visit requires a physician to listen to your lungs with a stethoscope or put their hands on your abdomen to diagnose some of these conditions … it makes no sense," Dr. Levy said. "Education about prevention, taking blood pressure, testing for hypertension, a lot of exams that don't require special training."

For Dr. Levy, the model also solved the physician shortage problem that plagues rural and underserved communities. Instead of requiring people to travel hours to see a doctor, mobile health could bring appropriate care to them.

The results were immediate and measurable. Using geospatial analysis, his team could target deployment to areas with the highest need. Blood pressure screenings that caught problems early. Diabetes education that prevented complications. Follow-up care that kept people healthy instead of waiting for them to get sick.

Dr. Levy's transformation from frustrated ER doctor to mobile health advocate represents his personal awakening to what healthcare could be. The pandemic had shown what was possible when you combined technology, community engagement, and preventive care. Now the question was whether others would see what he had seen.

"This is about the ability to get closer to clients and to get them thinking about healthcare in a very different way," Dr. Levy said. "This idea that we have to figure out workarounds for the inefficiencies of our healthcare system is silly. Why don't we instead come up with a system that makes more sense?"

The data supported his vision. Population health information could guide mobile site location. Blood pressure could be measured at scale, even in people's cars. Lab work could be done quickly and efficiently. The technology existed; what was missing was a pathway to fund it.

"It's not unreasonable to look at the expenditure on research and consider what return on investment we get for our money," Dr. Levy said. "The reality is that I'm at an academic institution, and I feel very strongly about research. But most government-funded research doesn't accomplish anything to change a patient's life or care. If you reconfigure some of those funds away from research and essentially dump that money into more mobile health, you're going to get a better outcome."

For Dr. Levy, the stakes couldn't be higher. Every day he could spend preventing the tragedies he'd witnessed was a day well spent. Every mobile clinic deployment was a chance to catch someone before they became his next patient.

"Mobile outreach and place-based engagement are poised to be at the leading edge of efficiency and operations. And I think it has a bright future," Dr. Levy said.

The future he envisioned wasn't just about better healthcare—it was about a fundamental shift from reactive to proactive care. Instead of waiting for people to get sick enough to need the ER, mobile health could catch problems early, when they were still treatable or preventable.

The ER doctor who had spent years watching preventable deaths had found a different way forward. For Dr. Levy, every prevented stroke, every controlled blood pressure, every caught-early diabetes case was a victory. It was healthcare as it should be: proactive, accessible, and focused on keeping people healthy rather than treating them when they were sick.

His revelation was complete, and he was no longer alone in his vision. He had joined our growing tribe of community clinicians, entrepreneurs, and advocates who understood that mobile health wasn't just an alternative—it was the future. There was work to be done, and now they could do it together.

Chapter 12

We Have Everything Except the Money

Dr. Jerry Isikoff has spent his career solving problems that others couldn't crack. Before he became CEO of the Infant Welfare Society of Chicago, which operates the Angel Harvey Family Health Center in Chicago's Logan Square neighborhood, he was the guy Humana called when its systems were failing its customers.

The problem was massive: thousands of complaints flooding in every month from frustrated patients trying to navigate an automated phone system that seemed designed to keep them away from help rather than connect them to it. Customer satisfaction scores were plummeting. The complaints kept coming. Something had to change.

Most executives would have looked for a technological solution—better software, more sophisticated routing, AI to handle the calls more efficiently. Isikoff, armed with a PhD in psychology and an intuitive understanding of human behavior, saw the problem differently.

"People who are sick are stressed," Isikoff explained. "They want to be heard, and they want to get answers, not navigate phone systems."

His solution was elegantly simple: Replace the automated system with human beings who could listen, understand, and respond to what patients needed. The complaints dropped from thousands to dozens almost overnight.

This lesson would shape everything Isikoff did next as he realized that, in healthcare, the human connection isn't just nice to have—it's essential. And when you remove that connection, you create problems that no amount of technology can solve.

The Infant Welfare Society of Chicago has been putting that philosophy into practice for more than a century through its flagship Angel Harvey Family Health Center. Founded over one hundred years ago, when Chicago was experiencing tremendous growth from immigration, the organization originally served families from Eastern Europe—Polish and Russian immigrants who were mostly poor, living together, scratching out a living in a new land.

Today, the faces have changed. The neighborhood is now home to Latino families and millennials, but the mission remains the same: Provide high-quality healthcare to everyone who walks through the door, regardless of their ability to pay.

For Isikoff, that mission requires something that can't be entered into a spreadsheet: trust. "Our neighborhood needs to hear us, they have to see us, and they have to feel like we hear and see them in return," he said. "They need to know we're human and that we care about them."

That trust doesn't come easy or quick. "The return on investment for community engagement is not something you'll see on a spreadsheet, and it's not a benefit you get overnight," Isikoff explained. "Our teams have incredible trust with our neighbors, but remember, that trust was built up over 115 years. When you have been somewhere for as long as we have, you don't just see patients from the same family—

you see generations of that family. We have children, grandchildren, and great-grandchildren who are coming to us."

It's the kind of institutional trust that can't be bought or manufactured. It must be earned, patient by patient, family by family, generation by generation.

But trust, Isikoff has learned, isn't enough if you can't reach the people who need you most.

The Angel Harvey Family Health Center serves a population that faces every barrier to healthcare access imaginable: language barriers, transportation challenges, work schedules that don't accommodate traditional clinic hours, immigration status fears, and financial constraints that make even subsidized care difficult to afford.

"There are so many patients who can't get to us," Isikoff said, "but we should always be trying to get to them."

During COVID-19, the Infant Welfare Society got a taste of what that could look like. It borrowed a mobile van from another organization to help distribute vaccinations in the community. The results were immediate and powerful.

"It was so incredibly useful," Isikoff said. "Being able to get information and vaccinations from someone who they trusted and had history with gave people such a sense of relief. The pandemic hammered home the reality to our team that there are so many patients who can't get to us, but we should always be trying to get to them."

The borrowed van wasn't just about convenience—it was about extending the trust and relationships the Infant Welfare Society had spent over a century building. When patients saw familiar faces from the Angel Harvey Center coming to their neighborhood, their workplace, their community gathering places, this removed barriers that went far beyond transportation.

The experience left Isikoff with a clear vision of what mobile health could accomplish and the realization that his organization had everything needed to make it work effectively.

Consider what the Infant Welfare Society brings to the table: 115 years of community trust that can't be replicated or bought. A staff of six hundred who understand the neighborhood intimately. Deep relationships with multiple generations of families. Bilingual capabilities that match the community's needs. Cultural competence built over decades of service. A health center designation that provides credibility and clinical expertise.

The organization also has the experience. The borrowed van during COVID-19 proved that mobile health works in its context. The society knows its community's barriers to access: transportation, work schedules, language, immigration fears, financial constraints. It knows exactly where to go and when to be there to reach the people who need it most.

"We know our community in ways that larger health systems simply can't," Isikoff said. "We've been here for over a century. We speak their languages, we understand their challenges, and most importantly, they trust us. When we show up with a mobile clinic, it's not some corporate outreach program—it's their healthcare home coming to them."

They have the vision. They have the relationships. They have the expertise. They have the community need. They have the trust.

What they don't have is the money.

"Mobile health is a multiplier," Isikoff said. "The things it would allow us to do—see people faster, connect with people who had the biggest risks, or even just distributing food … Whatever you're doing, having a mobile health program in your toolbox helps you accomplish it."

For a community health center serving a diverse, often marginalized population, mobile health could solve multiple problems at once. It could reach the undocumented workers who are afraid to come to a fixed clinic. It could serve the families in which parents work multiple jobs and can't take time off for appointments. It could bring preventive care to the elderly who struggle with transportation. It could provide health education in the languages and cultural contexts that make sense to different communities.

"Everyone wants a mobile health program," Isikoff continued. "We've considered all kinds of options. It's a problem solver. There are just so many opportunities."

But even with a staff of six hundred, the Infant Welfare Society depends on donations to survive. Isikoff and his team raise millions of dollars every year just to keep the doors open and the lights on. When everyone's plate is full of patients coming through the door, finding additional funding for mobile health feels almost impossible.

It's a cruel irony: The organizations that could most effectively use mobile health to serve vulnerable populations are often the ones with the least resources to implement it. Meanwhile, well-funded health systems that could easily afford mobile units often focus on profitable services rather than the unsexy work of preventive care and community outreach.

The mathematics of healthcare funding work against organizations like the one Isikoff led for decades. The programs traditionally require significant short-term investment—vehicles, equipment, staff, insurance, maintenance—but generate long-term returns in the form of prevented hospitalizations, improved community health outcomes, and stronger relationships with vulnerable populations. Those benefits are real and measurable, but they often accrue to the entire health system or community rather than to any specific organization making the investment.

For federally qualified health centers, such as the Angel Harvey Family Health Center, which already operate on razor-thin margins while serving the most complex and under-resourced patient populations, finding the capital for mobile health can seem impossible. Yet these are precisely the organizations that could use mobile health most effectively.

Isikoff sees this paradox clearly. "We have everything we need to make mobile health work except the funding," he said. "The trust, the relationships, the expertise, the community need—it's all there. We just need the resources to make it happen."

The frustration in his voice was palpable. It's the frustration of being ready to solve a problem but being held back by constraints beyond your control. It's like being the perfect candidate for a job you can't afford to take.

The Humana phone system story wasn't just about customer service—it was about recognizing that healthcare is fundamentally a human enterprise. When you remove the human connection, you create problems that technology alone can't solve. When you strengthen that connection, you create opportunities that extend far beyond the immediate interaction.

Mobile health, for Isikoff, represents the ultimate expression of that principle. It's healthcare that comes to people where they are, delivered by people they trust, designed around their needs rather than the convenience of the healthcare system.

"It's just like the complaint issue," Isikoff said. "A lot of the executives wanted that automated call service to save money, but it just didn't meet the needs of our clients."

The same principle applies to mobile health. It might seem more expensive up-front than waiting for people to come to you, but when you factor in the cost of emergency room visits, hospitalizations, and untreated chronic conditions, the economics change dramatically.

More importantly, the human impact changes everything. Instead of healthcare being something that happens to people when they're sick enough to overcome all the barriers to access, it becomes something that's woven into the fabric of their community life.

Isikoff's situation illustrates a fundamental problem in healthcare: readiness without resources. He's not dreaming about mobile health—he's working toward it, exploring partnerships with other organizations, looking for grant opportunities, and building the case with his board and donors.

"We're not just talking about it," he said. "We're working on it. Because we know what figuring out financial sustainability for these programs could mean for our communities and our country."

But the gap between what the organization could accomplish and what it can currently afford remains stark. The Infant Welfare Society's century-long commitment to its neighborhood has given it something that money can't buy: the trust and relationships that make mobile health truly effective. What it needs now is the resources to extend that trust beyond its walls.

This story repeats across the country. Community health centers and rural hospitals that have spent decades building exactly the kinds of relationships that make mobile health work are watching well-funded health systems deploy mobile units for profitable services while they struggle to find the resources to serve their vulnerable populations.

Isikoff, ever the problem solver, has identified the problems and the solution. He has assembled all the pieces except one. And that one missing piece—the funding—is the difference between a powerful vision and powerful action.

Chapter 13

The ROI Riddle—Solving Mobile Health's Funding Puzzle

As someone who has spent years building businesses and studying economics, I am drawn to the fundamental question that underlies every successful venture: Does this create more value than it costs? Studying business and economics in college, I was taught to look beyond primary effects, and my experience as an entrepreneur has shown me that the most important returns often come from places you don't expect.

When I first encountered mobile health, I was struck by the disconnect between the passionate advocates who knew it worked and the skeptical administrators who couldn't figure out how to pay for it.

That gap—between proven impact and practical funding—is familiar territory for anyone who has tried to scale a good idea in the real world. Policymakers and executives are attracted to the promise and potential of innovative solutions, but humans are risk averse, and the majority rarely do anything they haven't seen their peers do first.

The conversation always ends up at finance. In hundreds of conversations, I've explained how mobile health benefits a stack of stakeholders, shown data on positive outcomes and real returns in peer programs, plus all the predicted returns for their organization. People still look at me and say, "Yes, but how are we going to make a program pay for itself?"

Here's what I've learned about that skepticism: It's not personal, and it's not even about mobile health. It's normal. It's natural. Money is simply the language most people use to express their skepticism about the potential risk they see in a new solution.

Negativity bias—what psychologists Roy Baumeister and colleagues famously summarized as "Bad is stronger than good"—means humans are wired to give more weight to possible losses than possible gains.[29] When something new appears, the brain doesn't ask, "How could this help?" It asks, "What's the catch?" and "How much might it cost us?"

This instinct served our ancestors well on the savannah, but it makes introducing any innovation an uphill climb.

Ambiguity aversion compounds the problem. Economist Daniel Ellsberg demonstrated in 1961 that when people don't fully understand something, they often prefer the status quo—even when the status quo is clearly broken.[30] They'd rather stick with inefficient systems, long wait times, and overburdened hospitals than risk something unfamiliar that *might* be worse.

The result is that any proposed mobile healthcare program doesn't always get evaluated on its merits. It gets filtered through protective skepticism until the brain can fit it into a familiar category. This is the same resistance telehealth faced before COVID-19 forced rapid adoption, the same doubt that greeted urgent care centers and

29 Roy F. Baumeister et al., "Bad Is Stronger than Good," *Review of General Psychology* 5, no. 4 (2001): 323–70.

30 Daniel Ellsberg, "Risk, Ambiguity, and the Savage Axioms," *The Quarterly Journal of Economics* 75, no. 4 (1961): 643–69.

community paramedicine when they first emerged. The pattern is predictable. Understanding it doesn't make the resistance disappear, but it does change how we might respond to it.

Dr. Phil Levy encountered this question as he was putting together the COVID-19 programs and again when he was trialing his ideas for preventative care. This is the moment when aspirational (but theoretical) long-term benefits collide with practical operations folks and short-term budgets. Good intentions meet financial reality.

"You have to have dollars coming from somewhere to pay for this," Levy said. "I'm a great fan of how a lot of organizations come up with charity dollars and other ways to support mobile, but that's precarious, at best."

Despite the growing evidence that mobile health programs can generate significant returns, Levy put it bluntly: "Theoretical savings don't pay the bills."

This is the fundamental tension at the heart of health economics for this model. The benefits are real and measurable, but they often accrue to different stakeholders than those making the initial investment. The challenge isn't proving that mobile health works—it's proving that it works in ways that matter to the people who write the checks.

The Wrong-Pocket Problem

There are many definitions of ROI, and when it comes to debating decisions around investments in healthcare, not being aware of that fact is risky. In a world of scarce resources, every new thing must add value in some dimension that outweighs the costs.

The challenge that mobile health faces is in what economists call the wrong-pocket problem.

The wrong-pocket problem is a situation in which the costs of an intervention hit one budget while the benefits show up in completely different places. The organization making the investment doesn't capture all the returns, creating a fundamental misalignment of incentives.

This is also the reason adoption of mobile health is not more widespread; organizations that want to do the right thing often take on responsibility for investment and financial sustainability in a commoditized reimbursement scheme, while the system (insurance companies or government) realizes the return on that effort.

Nobel Prize–winning economist Kenneth Arrow recognized this phenomenon in his groundbreaking 1963 paper "Uncertainty and the Welfare Economics of Medical Care," in which he wrote, "When the market fails to achieve an optimal state, society will, to some extent at least, recognize the gap, and nonmarket social institutions will arise attempting to bridge it."[31]

Arrow's insight explains exactly what's happening with mobile health. The market failure isn't in the effectiveness of mobile health programs—it's in the alignment of costs and benefits. A community health center might invest in a mobile unit to prevent emergency room visits, but the savings accrue to hospitals and insurance companies. A health plan might fund mobile clinics to improve chronic disease management, but the productivity gains and reduced absenteeism benefit employers and the broader economy.

The return isn't always financial. What's the differential ROI on someone spending more on a first-class seat versus a coach-class seat? It adds value, but not financial value.

31 Kenneth J. Arrow, "Uncertainty and the Welfare Economics of Medical Care," *The American Economic Review* 53, no. 5 (1963): 941–73.

The return isn't always short term. What's the value of a college education? It doesn't have a two-year payback, but data shows it returns significant value to a graduate and their future family over many decades.

But system savings calculation will not solve the funding problem for individual organizations. As Levy said, "You have to think about funding from the perspective of whoever is paying the bill; it's as simple as that."

Or, as I like to say, "In the return on investment calculation, make sure everyone who is involved in the *R* is also involved in the *I*."

For a complete picture of mobile health's economic impact, we can examine four distinct types of ROI that any robust net benefit calculation must recognize: direct short-term financial returns, direct long-term financial returns, indirect long-term financial returns, and long-term organizational returns.

Direct Short-Term Financial Returns

UNNECESSARY EMERGENCY ROOM VISITS

Whether it's in rural areas or cities, when people experience what they consider serious health situations and cannot get care elsewhere for some reason, they will go to the emergency room.

Many times, their complaint could have been prevented with better access to basic healthcare or through preventative medicine. Oftentimes, their illnesses would be better taken care of in a doctor's office. But they opt for an ER because, there in the moment, in their mind, there is no alternative. Even the most hard-nosed MBA healthcare administrator can admit, no one goes to the ER for fun.

This paradigm costs Americans hundreds of millions of dollars each year in higher costs and inefficient use of taxpayer dollars. For example, UnitedHealth Group reports that the average cost of treating ten common primary care treatable conditions at a hospital ED is $2,032, around $1,800 higher per visit than a primary care visit.[32]

The numbers are stark: A 2011–2013 study of the Oregon All Payer All Claims database shows approximately 44.5 percent of Medicaid patients visited the ED at least once a year, about four times more than non-Medicaid patients. Research consistently finds that a substantial portion of ED visits are for conditions treatable in primary care settings.[33]

One survey found 45.3 percent of adult Medicaid enrollees presenting to the ED with low acuity conditions would have "preferred to use their PCP rather than the ED, if an appointment had been immediately available."[34]

Patient respondent data from Harvard Medical School's The Family Van program suggests that up to 27 percent of all visits to a mobile clinic represent avoided ED visits. If we could prevent even a fraction of these unnecessary ED visits, the savings would be immediate and substantial.[35]

---

32 J. P. Williams, "Avoidable ER Visits Fuel U.S. Health Care Costs," *U.S. News & World Report*, July 22, 2019, https://www.usnews.com/news/health-news/articles/2019-07-22/avoidable-er-visits-fuel-us-health-care-costs.

33 Hyunjee Kim et al., "Comparing Emergency Department Use Among Medicaid and Commercial Patients Using All-Payer All-Claims Data," *Journal of General Internal Medicine* 32, no. 5 (2017): 539–45.

34 Roberta Capp et al., "Do Adult Medicaid Enrollees Prefer Going to Their Primary Care Provider's Clinic Rather Than Emergency Department (ED) for Low Acuity Conditions?" *Medical Care* 53, no. 6 (2015): 530–33.

35 Zirui Song et al., "Mobile Clinic in Massachusetts Associated with Cost Savings from Lowering Blood Pressure and Emergency Department Use," *Health Affairs* 32, no. 1 (2013): 36–44.

THE MATERNAL HEALTH CRISIS

Despite post-COVID-19 declines, the US suffers the highest maternal mortality rate among high-income nations, with rates highest for Black women. Over 80 percent of these deaths are preventable.[36]

Among women without timely prenatal care, maternal mortality risk increases three- to four-fold; infant death rates increase five-fold.[37] The economic impact is equally dramatic: Average hospital charges for low-birth-weight infants reach $39,704, while very-low-birth-weight infants cost $111,960 (inflation adjusted from 2011 data).[38]

The cost escalation is exponential. A 2019 study of California births (2009–2011 data) indicated the mean cost for all newborns was $6,389: $2,433 for term infants, $22,102 for late preterm infants, $223,931 for very preterm infants, and $317,982 for extremely preterm infants (less than twenty-eight weeks old).[39]

The economic case for maternal health interventions is particularly compelling because of pregnancy's unique timeline. Unlike many healthcare investments that require years to show returns, improvements in prenatal and postpartum care can demonstrate measurable impact within the nine-month pregnancy cycle. This means that maternal health programs can contribute to short-term savings within a typical three- to five-year contract term, making them especially

---

36 Munira Z. Gunja et al., "Insights into the U.S. Maternal Mortality Crisis: An International Comparison," *Commonwealth Fund*, June 4, 2024, www.commonwealthfund.org/publications/issue-briefs/2024/jun/insights-us-maternal-mortality-crisis-international-comparison.

37 California Department of Health Care Services, "Prenatal and Postpartum Care," accessed February 12, 2026, https://www.dhcs.ca.gov/dataandstats/Pages/PrenatalandPostpartumCare.aspx.

38 Niranjana M. Kowlessar et al., "Hospital Stays for Newborns, 2011," *HCUP Statistical Brief #163*, Agency for Healthcare Research and Quality, October 2013.

39 Ciaran S. Phibbs et al., "Birth Hospitalization Costs and Days of Care for Mothers and Neonates in California, 2009–2011," *Journal of Pediatrics* 204 (2019): 118–25.

attractive to health plans and policymakers who need to show results quickly. The cost differential between healthy deliveries and complicated births involving preterm or low-birth-weight infants creates substantial opportunities for ROI when preventive care is accessible.

MEDICATION RECONCILIATION

The prevalence of polypharmacy in the Medicaid population (the simultaneous use of five or more different drug classes for a sixty-day consecutive period) has been identified as 50.9 percent.[40] Prior research shows that approximately 50 percent of adults with a chronic illness do not take their medications as prescribed.[41]

In one study of 851 adults hospitalized with acute coronary syndrome or acute decompensated heart failure, 432 (50.8 percent) experienced one or more clinically important medication errors; nearly 23 percent of the errors were judged to be serious.[42]

Mobile health programs can address this through systematic "brown bag reviews," in which patients bring all their medications to the provider for reconciliation and simplification. Researchers suggest the cost savings from avoided readmissions more than offset the cost of systematic intervention. In one study, medication reconciliation

40 Xue Feng et al., "Polypharmacy and Multimorbidity Among Medicaid Enrollees: A Multistate Analysis," *Population Health Management* 21, no. 2 (2018): 123–29.

41 Marie T. Brown and Jennifer K. Bussell, "Medication Adherence: WHO Cares?" *Mayo Clinic Proceedings* 86, no. 4 (2011): 304–14.

42 Sunil Kripalani et al., "Effect of a Pharmacist Intervention on Clinically Important Medication Errors After Hospital Discharge: A Randomized Trial," *Annals of Internal Medicine* 157, no. 1 (2012): 1–10.

interventions completed at a community teaching hospital avoided an estimated $46,958 to $231,032 in additional costs in just thirty days.[43]

Mobile health programs are uniquely positioned to deliver on all three of these short-term financial promises. By bringing primary care directly to underserved communities, mobile clinics eliminate many of the transportation and access barriers preventing primary care that then result in unnecessary emergency room visits.

The regular rotation through rural areas ensures that pregnant women can receive consistent prenatal care close to home, preventing the complications that lead to costly preterm births. And the systematic medication reconciliation services—conducting brown bag reviews during mobile clinic visits—address polypharmacy issues before they result in hospitalizations. Unlike traditional healthcare delivery models that require patients to navigate multiple systems and locations, mobile health consolidates these high-impact interventions into a single, accessible platform.

This integration doesn't just improve health outcomes; it creates immediate, measurable cost savings that flow directly to the organizations smart enough to invest in the model.

Direct Long-Term Financial Returns

THE CHRONIC DISEASE CHALLENGE

Over time, expanding access to convenient, affordable primary care is expected to significantly and sustainably improve at least three chronic conditions: hypertension, diabetes, and chronic kidney disease (CKD).

---

43 Abigail M. Hoffman et al., "Prevented Harm and Cost Avoidance with Pharmacist Intervention While Utilizing a Discharge Medication Reconciliation Tool," *American Journal of Health-System Pharmacy* 81, no. 1 (2024): e37–e44.

The economic impact of these improvements compounds over years.

HYPERTENSION CONTROL

Hypertension affects approximately 35 percent of Medicaid beneficiaries. The cost of uncontrolled hypertension increases dramatically with each additional comorbidity, with estimated individual healthcare costs ranging from $5,500 to $19,000 annually.[44]

The American Heart Association states the potential for reducing total cost of care by controlling hypertension and avoiding heart conditions is significant. Cardiac catheterization costs $54,000 per event; pacemaker implantations are $80,000 each. Bypass and valve surgeries are $160,000 and $193,000, respectively.[45]

DIABETES MANAGEMENT

The Kaiser Commission reports that the prevalence of diabetes mellitus in the Medicaid population is 9 percent, and average annual spending by Medicaid adults with diabetes is 2.5 times the amount of those without diabetes ($13,490).[46]

The cost of medical care increases significantly for every 1 percent increase in a patient's glycemic level (for HbA1c above 7 percent). A study of 77,622 people with diabetes found that a 1 percent

---

44 John M. Chapel et al. "Prevalence and Medical Costs of Chronic Diseases Among Adult Medicaid Beneficiaries," *American Journal of Preventive Medicine* 53, no. 6 (2017): 143–54.

45 Wayne Rosamond et al., "Heart Disease and Stroke Statistics—2008 Update: A Report from the American Heart Association Statistics Committee and Stroke Statistics Subcommittee," *Circulation* 117, no. 4 (2007).

46 Kaiser Commission on Medicaid and the Uninsured, *The Role of Medicaid for People with Diabetes* (Henry J. Kaiser Family Foundation, 2012).

improvement in HbA1c was associated with a 13 percent drop in diabetes-related costs—roughly $555 per patient per year.[47]

CHRONIC KIDNEY DISEASE PREVENTION

The National Kidney Foundation estimates that one in every three adults—some eighty million people—is at risk for CKD. It is the ninth leading cause of death in the US, killing more people than breast cancer or prostate cancer every year.

The economic modeling for CKD prevention is particularly compelling. In a population of approximately two thousand Medicaid members, systematically reducing CKD progression by 30 percent is predictive of cost savings of around $1.3 million annually. This is because annual all-cause costs for CKD increase dramatically as the disease advances, from $26,843 per year for moderate CKD to $76,969 per year for advanced stages.

Mobile health programs excel at generating direct long-term financial returns because they cost-effectively address the root causes of expensive chronic conditions before they become insanely costly to treat.

By establishing regular touchpoints with underserved populations, mobile clinics create the consistent care relationships necessary for effective chronic disease management—catching diabetes before it progresses to dialysis, managing hypertension before it leads to heart failure, and ensuring cancer screenings happen before conditions become terminal. The childhood immunization programs delivered through mobile units prevent not just individual cases of measles or

---

47 Michael J. Lage and Kristina S. Boye, "The Relationship Between HbA1c Reduction and Healthcare Costs Among Patients with Type 2 Diabetes: Evidence from a U.S. Claims Database," *Current Medical Research and Opinion* 36, no. 9 (2020): 1441–47.

whooping cough, but also the community-wide outbreaks that can cost health systems millions in emergency response.

Most importantly, mobile health programs institutionalize early detection in communities that traditionally receive care only after conditions have progressed to crisis stages. This systematic approach to prevention transforms the long-term cost trajectory for entire populations, creating sustainable savings that compound year after year. The mobile model doesn't just deliver healthcare—it delivers the consistency and accessibility that preventive care requires to generate meaningful long-term returns.

Indirect Long-Term Financial Returns

Indirect long-term financial returns represent the economic benefits that mobile health programs generate for organizations and systems beyond the direct healthcare delivery network. These returns are often the largest in magnitude but the most difficult to capture for the organizations making the initial investment.

EMPLOYER BENEFITS FROM HEALTHIER COMMUNITIES

When mobile health programs improve population health in a community, local employers see significant indirect returns through reduced absenteeism, lower workers' compensation claims, and decreased healthcare premiums. A mobile clinic that provides regular blood pressure monitoring and diabetes management doesn't just prevent individual heart attacks and strokes—it can create a healthier workforce that shows up to work more consistently and requires fewer sick days.

Rural employers particularly benefit when mobile health programs eliminate the need for workers to take full days off for medical appointments that might require travel to distant healthcare facilities. The productivity gains from having healthy, present employees often exceed the direct medical cost savings.

SCHOOL DISTRICT BENEFITS FROM HEALTHIER STUDENTS

Mobile health programs that serve children create substantial indirect returns for school districts through improved attendance, better academic performance, and reduced burden on school nurses and counselors. When mobile clinics provide regular vision and hearing screenings, they identify learning barriers early, preventing years of educational struggles that might otherwise require expensive special education interventions.

Childhood obesity prevention programs delivered through mobile units reduce the long-term healthcare costs that school districts face as self-insured entities.

Mental health services provided through mobile platforms help identify and address behavioral issues before they escalate into disciplinary problems that disrupt entire classrooms.

INSURANCE COMPANY QUALITY MEASURE BENEFITS

For insurance companies, mobile health programs represent an opportunity to improve quality measures that directly impact their revenue through government bonus payments and competitive ratings. Medicare Advantage plans receive substantial financial incentives for achieving high scores on measures such as blood pressure control, diabetes management, and cancer screening rates—exactly the services that mobile health programs excel at delivering to hard-to-reach populations.

A mobile clinic that improves medication adherence rates or increases mammography screening participation can generate hundreds of thousands of dollars in quality bonuses for health plans. These quality measure improvements also enhance plan ratings, which drive member enrollment and retention in competitive markets.

COMMUNITY ECONOMIC DEVELOPMENT

Mobile health programs contribute to broader economic development by making communities more attractive to businesses and families. Areas with reliable healthcare access see increased property values, business investment, and population retention. When mobile health programs reduce the burden on EDs, they free up hospital resources for more profitable procedures and services.

The clinical data generated by mobile health programs also creates valuable population health intelligence that can inform community development and policy decisions.

GOVERNMENT FISCAL BENEFITS

State and local governments see reduced Medicaid costs, decreased reliance on safety-net programs, and increased tax revenue from healthier working populations who remain employed longer. When mobile health programs prevent disabilities and premature deaths, they reduce the burden on public assistance programs and increase the tax base.

SOCIAL SERVICES COST REDUCTION

Mobile health programs that address mental health, substance abuse, and family health issues can significantly reduce costs for child protective services, disability services, and elderly care programs. Early intervention through mobile platforms often prevents family crises that require expensive social service interventions.

CRIMINAL JUSTICE SYSTEM IMPACT

There's substantial research showing connections between untreated mental health issues, substance abuse, and incarceration rates. Mobile health programs that provide mental health services and addiction treatment can reduce recidivism and the associated costs of policing, courts, and corrections.

HIGHER EDUCATION COMPLETION

Healthier students are more likely to pursue and complete higher education, generating long-term economic returns through increased earning potential and reduced reliance on social services. This is particularly significant for first-generation college students from underserved communities.

AGRICULTURAL ECONOMY SUPPORT

In rural areas, mobile health programs that keep farmers and agricultural workers healthy support the entire agricultural economy, preventing disruptions to food production and maintaining rural economic stability.

THE BEHAVIORAL HEALTH FACTOR

The indirect returns extend to behavioral health as well. Studies consistently find that interventions for mental health prevention and promotion are cost-effective or cost saving.[48]

A January 2023 study found that first-year medical and pharmacy cost savings occurred among people with at least one outpatient visit with a behavioral health provider. The fifteen-month cost savings were, on average, between $915 and $2,565 per person.[49]

The research findings are particularly relevant for people living with co-occurring behavioral and physical health conditions. Healthcare costs for this population can be two to six times greater than for those without a behavioral health condition.[50] Authors calculate that between 9 percent and 17 percent of the excess costs incurred by individuals with comorbid physical and behavioral health conditions might be saved through effective integration of medical and behavioral care.

RETURNS THAT RIPPLE

The economic case for mobile health extends far beyond traditional healthcare cost–benefit calculations. When we trace the full impact of bringing accessible healthcare directly to underserved communities, we see returns flowing to EDs, health plans, employers, school districts, insurance companies, government agencies, social services,

48 Long Khanh-Dao Le et al., "Cost-Effectiveness Evidence of Mental Health Prevention and Promotion Interventions: A Systematic Review of Economic Evaluations," *PLOS Medicine* 18, no. 5 (2021).

49 Evernorth Health Services, *Impact of Behavioral Health Treatment on Total Medical and Pharmacy Costs* (Evernorth Health Services, 2023).

50 Davenport et al., *How Do Individuals with Behavioral Health Conditions Contribute to Physical and Total Healthcare Spending?* (Milliman, 2020).

criminal justice systems, higher education institutions, and entire regional economies.

Mobile health programs simultaneously reduce immediate costs through emergency room avoidance and medication reconciliation while building long-term savings through chronic disease prevention and early detection. They create healthier workforces that boost productivity, healthier students who achieve better educational outcomes, and healthier communities that attract business investment and population growth. They reduce the burden on social services, decrease recidivism rates, and support economic stability in rural areas.

The returns then compound across sectors and generations. A program that prevents childhood obesity doesn't just save future healthcare costs—it improves educational outcomes, increases lifetime earning potential, reduces disability payments, and strengthens entire communities. A mental health program doesn't just prevent individual crises—it reduces family disruption, decreases incarceration rates, and enables higher education completion.

The question isn't whether mobile health programs can generate positive returns on investment. The evidence clearly demonstrates they can. The question is, *What if enhanced community healthcare, such as mobile health programs, could produce even a fraction of these benefits?*

Given the scope of potential returns across multiple sectors and the relatively modest investment required, can we afford not to scale these programs to serve every underserved community?

Long-Term Organizational Returns

Health economists also consider indirect long-term organizational returns—such as stronger quality ratings, risk score improvement, member retention, and brand equity—important components of robust net benefit calculations.

THE COMPETITIVE ADVANTAGE

The strategic implications are significant. For a health system or health plan, a reliable, data-driven system of care that controls total cost of care in rural communities represents what business strategists would call a sustainable competitive advantage—difficult to replicate and valuable over time.

What Michael Porter calls sustainable competitive advantage—a capability that creates value and resists imitation—describes precisely what a mature mobile health operation provides.[51]

A well-developed rural strategy also supports strategic imperatives, such as de-risking contract renewals and supporting entry into new markets in which one may have zero existing operations and is building everything—including licenses, provider contracts, sales channels, and brand awareness—from the ground up.

RISK ADJUSTMENT AND REVENUE ENHANCEMENT

For health plans, mobile health programs can generate direct revenue enhancements through improved risk redeterminations in "unable to reach" member cohorts. A 2022 KFF survey of twenty-nine Medicaid managed care plans serving over 13.2 million beneficiaries found that nearly all responding plans said regularly reaching Medicaid beneficiaries is a challenge, and only about one-third reported

51 Michael E. Porter, *Competitive Advantage: Creating and Sustaining Superior Performance* (Free Press, 1985).

having verified contact information for more than 75 percent of their members.[52]

When chronic conditions go undiagnosed, risk for acute episodes accumulates over time without the accompanying offset of accurate risk revenue. Financial modeling suggests that in a population of two thousand members, accurate redetermination of just fifty high-risk members could result in approximately $210,000 in additional annual revenue, recurring over the contract's remaining years.

INSURANCE COMPANY QUALITY MEASURE BENEFITS

For insurance companies, mobile health programs represent an opportunity to improve quality measures that directly impact revenue through government bonus payments and competitive ratings. Medicare Advantage plans receive substantial financial incentives for achieving high scores on measures such as blood pressure control, diabetes management, and cancer screening rates—exactly the services that mobile health programs excel at delivering to hard-to-reach populations. A mobile clinic that improves medication adherence or increases mammography screening can generate hundreds of thousands of dollars in quality bonuses while enhancing plan ratings that drive member enrollment and retention.

52 Elizabeth Hinton et al., "Understanding the Role of Medicaid Managed Care Plans in Unwinding Pandemic-Era Continuous Enrollment: Perspectives from Safety-Net Plans," *KFF*, February 13, 2023, https://www.kff.org/medicaid/understanding-the-role-of-medicaid-managed-care-plans-in-unwinding-pandemic-era-continuous-enrollment-perspectives-from-safety-net-plans/.

THE QUALITY IMPROVEMENT WITHHOLD OPPORTUNITY

The scale of this opportunity is staggering. Hundreds of millions of dollars in quality improvement withholds remain locked away because current healthcare delivery models cannot reach the populations needed to move quality metrics. Rural beneficiaries who can't access regular care, urban populations facing transportation barriers, and working families who can't take time off for appointments represent the missing pieces that prevent health plans from unlocking these massive financial incentives.

Mobile health programs are uniquely positioned to capture these withheld funds by eliminating access barriers that prevent quality measure achievement. When a mobile clinic parks outside a senior housing complex to provide on-site blood pressure monitoring, diabetes management, and medication reviews, it moves population-level quality metrics that trigger millions in bonus payments. For major health plans managing hundreds of thousands of members, even modest improvements in quality scores could translate to tens of millions in additional revenue. The business case becomes compelling when health plans realize that comprehensive mobile health programs often cost a fraction of the quality bonuses they could unlock—accessing revenue streams that are currently beyond reach through conventional healthcare delivery.

The Bottom Line

The economic case for mobile health is complex because its benefits are multifaceted. Direct short-term savings from avoided ED visits and prevented complications are measurable and immediate. Long-term savings from chronic disease management compound over years. Indirect returns from improved population health and productivity are real but harder to quantify. Organizational returns from competitive advantage and quality improvement are strategic but significant.

The challenge isn't proving that mobile health generates returns—it's aligning those returns with the stakeholders who can fund the initial investment. When that alignment happens, the nineteen-to-one ROI that Dr. Oriol calculated becomes not just a theoretical benefit, but a practical reality.

The economics show that mobile health is a solution that pays for itself, just not always in the abbreviated fashion focused on short-term and direct financial returns that shortcut ROI calculations routinely produce.

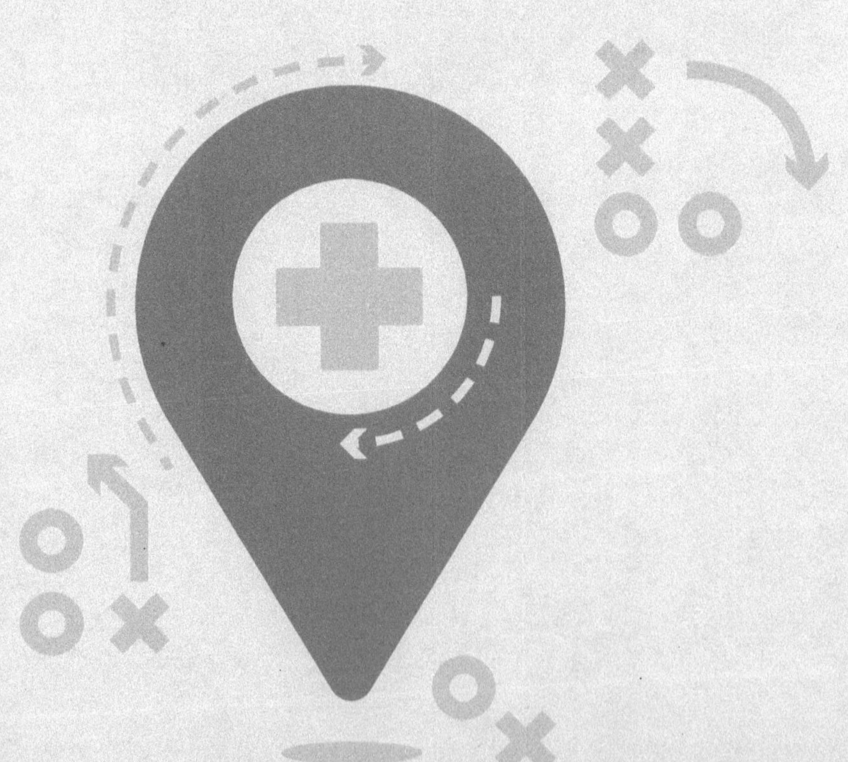

Chapter 14
Wildfires, Farmworkers, and Football

One of the great values of mobile health is the opportunity to be nimble. From the ability to pick up and move to a new location or make changes in the type of care that's provided from one place to another, the mobile model provides an unprecedented versatility—especially in an emergency.

Dr. Rosemary Reyes, the chief executive officer at Central City Community Health Center, Inc. (CCCHC) in Monterey Park, California, discovered just how important mobile healthcare could be in one of the most unprecedented moments in Los Angeles history. Central City is in the far east part of Los Angeles and just inside the rim of the San Gabriel Valley.

In January 2025, the Altadena area just to the north of where the main office is located was one of the hardest hit by a series of wildfires that dotted Los Angeles from Central City to the eastern part of the city to the coastline in Malibu. The city was literally under siege from a combination of drought conditions, overgrown brush, and dry Santa Ana winds that whipped at upward of one hundred miles per hour.

The conditions were so bad that dark clouds carried ash upward of twenty miles away to the southwestern parts of Los Angeles. Hundreds of homes were destroyed in an area that had been hit hard only two years before by other fires. Worse, upward of four hundred people died, either directly from the fire or from associated events.

For Dr. Reyes, the problem was basic. The fires burned down eight of the seventeen clinics that CCCHC operated in the four-county area (the Los Angeles, Orange, Riverside, and San Bernardino counties). CCCHC, which has operated in Southern California since 1994, is a critical provider for many of the underserved patients in Southern California, including a large swath of the Latino community.

With people struggling to get anywhere and with many people impacted by breathing the soot-filled air, Dr. Reyes needed to put every one of the six mobile clinics the organization owns to work and to do it quickly. Any unit that was a specialty vehicle was now converted into general use. The vehicles were always on the road, meeting the needs of patients who desperately needed them.

"For us to continue providing that access of care was to mobilize our mobile units," Dr. Reyes said. "We just had a meeting with a couple of donors and said this is what we have to do to take of our people. We gave them a tour of our mobile units and the burn sites and they were just thrilled that that access of care was not affected because, at the end of the day, the rebuilding and restructuring of patient homes and facilities takes a very, very long time. And even in that area, they're just barely getting the hazardous material out. There are still a lot of dump trucks driving around town.

"The whole neighborhood is still shut down. There are not a lot of buildings. And so, it's a long process. But at the same token, you know, healthcare doesn't stop, right? If we can't have a structure, the mobiles are our way to do it."

This is one of the great examples of how one organization was able to flip the use of mobile models from one use case to another. And this is yet another example of ROI to build on the economics of mobile health. This chapter discusses several ways organizations add value with mobile healthcare. But for the moment, we'll stay in Los Angeles with Dr. Reyes and CCCHC.

Farmworkers in California

Dr. Reyes and CCCHC have also used their mobile programs to become more profitable in other areas so that they can carry out the mission of the organization to take care of migrant workers. The best example Dr. Reyes had was her organization's ability to use mobile health programming for its residential care facilities. CCCHC provides care without having to pay for additional physical overhead.

"We go there and we provide sort of concierge medicine to each person in that setting because these patients are duly diagnosed. They have chronic diseases; these are patients that are likely (convalescent), that require podiatry, primary care, psychiatry, and so we bring medicine to them."

CCCHC serves approximately six hundred facilities, meaning that the overhead for that care could be potentially astronomical if the organization had to rent space from each company.

"Imagine having that overhead," Dr. Reyes said. "And imagine not having to pay for utilities or any of that. It's just really our staff that we're paying for … to see those patients that are uninsured, see the patients in the community, without requiring them being our own patients.

"These are not buildings that we own, so we would have to rent out space in a more traditional setting without the mobile units. But now we can bring out a full staff and get people taken care of while billing at a better rate. That leaves us the ability to do the other parts of our organization's mission without having to stress as much about having to pay for it.

"It was such an important time for us because the mobile units definitely have the capacity to bring patients the care that they need, and it's exciting to see that. We're growing as an organization, but also there's definitely still areas in the community where we can bring medicine to them. We go out regularly and participate in the community in health fairs."

Farmworkers in Georgia

Another great use of mobile healthcare is in Georgia, where Share Health Southeast provides healthcare after dark.

Share Health sets up shop near farms in the southeast part of the state. Migrant workers come throughout the year to work the farms and harvest the sweet Vidalia onions that grow in this part of the world. Setting up at night is critical for the migrant workers (and particularly for their children), who find it almost impossible to get away from work.

For Share Health, the person who makes sure the operation is as effective and efficient as possible is Peyton Frye, a former senior vice president at Spivey State Bank in Georgia who left the financial sector for something more meaningful.

Frye understands why some mobile health programs are more financially successful than others. He honed his outreach and engagement skills over decades in the local banking industry before entering healthcare, and he has effectively employed those skills during his time with Share Health.

He is always asking questions about how people use mobile clinics. He sees other healthcare organizations that spend a lot of time and money on community events promoting their organization—sponsoring golf tournaments or health fairs—but notes those organizations often don't think to bring their mobile unit with them, missing the easy marketing opportunity.

Frye said he'll get approached about sponsoring a golf tournament and often will double down on the sponsorship opportunity if he is given a chance. Instead of paying only $150 to be a sponsor at a local event, he said he'll pay $300 if the event allows him to park his mobile health team on or near the golf course or at the place where people will gather after they are done.

"It's a free billboard wherever you can get it," he said. "Especially if there's a spot near the road where I can park the mobile unit, I'm going to sponsor it. That's the lowest-hanging fruit." Not only that, but it's a great way to introduce the care team to the community.

For Frye, working to help people in the area near where he grew up and went to college was something of a calling. He attended Valdosta State, in the heart of Southeast Georgia, near the farms where migrants pick onions and families work the land, growing peanuts and other crops. It's a special place for him not only because he grew up there but also because of the immense pride the community has for Vidalia onions. There's reason to be proud; between the soil and the weather, the onion simply doesn't grow the same way in any other part of the world, and the sweetness is synonymous with numerous Southern dishes.

Like so many regions of the United States (and the world, generally), those areas that grow specific crops also become somewhat economically dependent on the crop. The area in and around Valdosta was also a major cotton producer for centuries. But as cotton prices have dropped because of worldwide production and peanut prices fluctuate year to year, there has been a further shift toward producing Vidalia onions because of the profit margins.

In turn, protecting all the parts of that value stream is vital. One element is ensuring that the workforce is healthy. Share Health's efforts to improve access, availability, and convenience are essential to the local economy.

Frye is passionately tied to that idea. Doing his part to support that part of the area's culture and economy is a point of pride and tradition. Share Health's mobile health programs are critical to making the equation work.

"That's so important for us in using it for outreach in a migrant seasonal population," Frye said.

"We're four miles off the main road down a dirt road at some barracks for migrant season farmworkers. This is 90 percent men who are out here working ... but it's really like a fraternity house with no money. That's the only way I can describe it."

The barracks are sometimes as simple as block buildings with three drains in the middle of the floor. There are showers and some restrooms, but overall, it's primitive. That is a giant public health challenge, as germs and viruses spread through the population.

Share Health travels hundreds of miles during the harvest season to serve workers, setting up a primary care clinic night after night. Frye helped organize it all—every night, temporary light carts cut through the darkness of the parking lots as his care teams see thousands of workers for checkups, immunizations, and other care.

"We see about four thousand individual, unduplicated patients in the fields in the evenings and on the weekends. We get a large influx of H-2A workers. They come up from Florida, the Miami area, to pick food crops. That's part of our business model, for sure."

Healthy High School Athletes

In the football-loving South, Frye found another solid way to add value to the community with the mobile health program while creating a solid source of consistent income: school sports.

Without a hint of hesitation, Frye will tell you, "Your best way to make sure you've got business is to be working with middle schools and high schools, and your best friends in that school are the football coach, the basketball coach, the baseball coach, and the band director. Those coaches and directors want their kids to be healthy, and healthy every day. Moreover, those people will help you make sure that the student heads to the clinic the minute the student doesn't feel good."

Sick visits and immunizations are on top of the annual requirements for high school athletes to get physicals at the beginning of every season. Sports physicals are perfectly suited for a mobile health program and are convenient because these visits can be done anytime the student-athlete is on campus. Coupled with the fact that physicals can be paid through Medicaid, this becomes another consistent source of income for a healthcare organization and helps ensure operating revenue exceeds expenses.

Likewise, game-day support provides some opportunities to engage. Frye said that if the school doesn't have a team doctor, much of the medical care the athletes need can be supported by the mobile programs, such as hydrating athletes on hot days or treating pulled muscles post-game. "When it's hot down here and you're doing things that keep the trainers from dealing with cramping, they love it."

In addition to the reimbursements for medical services and occasional booster club support, every game is an opportunity for community engagement and adds to the goodwill the program generates in the community.

"So, it's a great thing you can do to involve yourself in the community. The coaches love you; the trainers love you. The parents are happy; the athletes are happy. You get free sponsors. We have a top-tier sponsorship at the local high school, and we've paid exactly zero dollars for that because of the services we provide, even though we are charging for the services," said Frye, who made a pledge the first year to never charge a student-athlete on an individual basis.

Instead, Frye has always found a way to bill for the services. At first, he was concerned about whether that would work, but it has always settled itself. That has allowed the outreach program to be extremely successful in terms of both paying for services and forging a stronger relationship with the community. Finally, it has helped capture the attention of those athletes who eventually grow to be lifetime patients.

The value for Share Health is that, as the school programs grow, their patient count continues to skyrocket. With each new class of students, Share Health is adding roughly three hundred students. The program that Frye came up with was so successful that Share Health was able to start a second mobile health program with equipment repurposed from another organization.

School-Based Health in Florida

A more traditional example of school-based programming is PanCare, in Panama City, Florida.

PanCare operates an enterprise mobile health program that helps more than fourteen thousand children per year using eleven separate programs. Those fourteen thousand children complete more than thirty thousand visits per year.

"We've had a mobile program since I started in 2013," Robert Thompson, CEO of PanCare said. "When I started, we had one mobile dental unit that just did some part-time work in the school district here locally. But as of today, we've got mobile medical, mobile dental, behavioral health, and optometry."

When Thompson arrived at PanCare, the mobile health program was focused on community health, but he quickly changed that focus of pediatric care. Over the years, PanCare has developed partnerships with local schools that allow for sustainable programming, sequencing initial visits and follow-up exams.

The system is particularly important for optometry appointments.

Prior to PanCare fully developing the mobile optometry program, children would receive vision screenings, and some would indicate a problem. However, when coordinating follow-up exams was left to the parents, obstacles would surface, and those visits would often be forgotten. Many parents didn't have the time or money for those follow-ups.

"The school district kept reporting back to us that they had a high, high noncompliance rate with parents who would not follow up on the vision screening failures," Thompson said. "Our solution was, let's just try and buy a mobile optometry clinic and get an optometrist."

Follow-up visits could then be coordinated on-site so that kids who failed the initial vision screening would immediately go to the optometrist and pick from their frames. They would get fitted with the right lenses, and the completed glasses would arrive at school shortly after.

"They go from failing a screen to having a solution right away," Thompson said.

These and many more examples of successful mobile health programs surround us. They operate at varying levels of complexity and success. Some collect data, conduct formal evaluations, and carefully design for financial sustainability. Others are satisfied with hugs and hearty handshakes when they provide that overdue checkup or a discounted prescription or simply listen to someone's concerns about their health.

There is no "right" way to help people, and there is no "right" way to run a mobile health program. No book about people who were leading the way would be complete without mentioning these leaders and their programs.

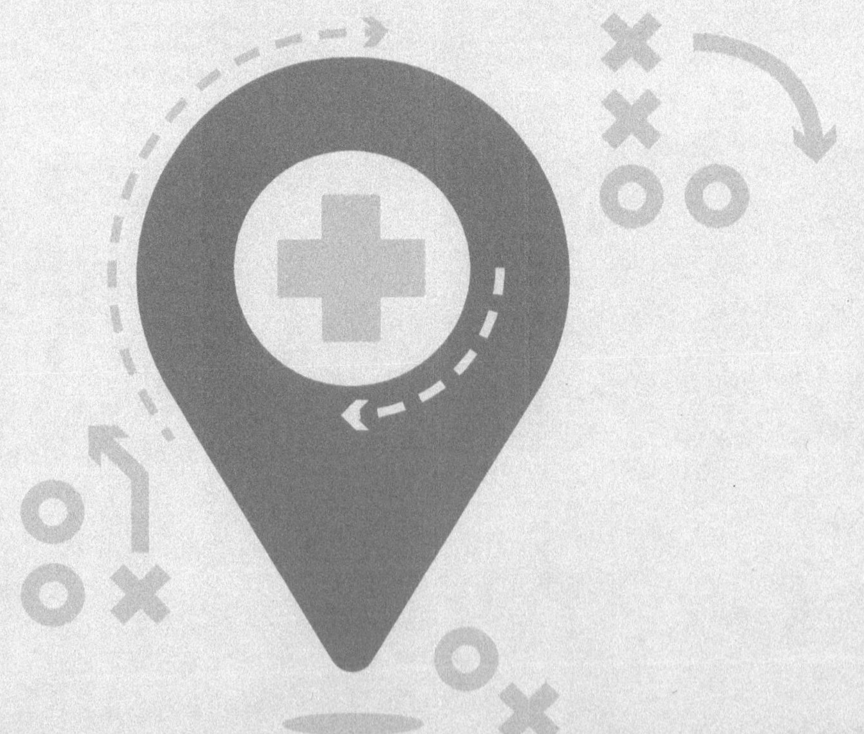

PART 3

Mobile Health Tomorrow

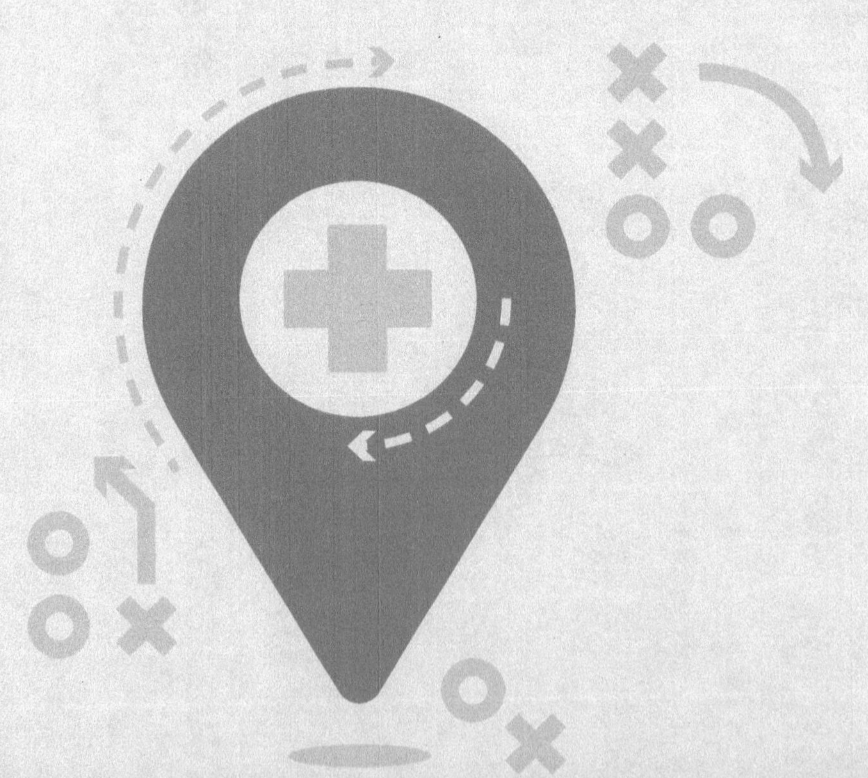

Chapter 15

Mobile Health 2030

As healthcare solutions are built, it's normal and expected that version 1.0 isn't always the best. Version 2.0 is better, and as 3.0 comes around, the next breakthrough is already in testing or trials, on its way to market. Change is constant.

Also, it's normal and expected that change can be slow and messy. Successful implementation of medical breakthroughs regularly takes years (if not decades), costs much more than originally planned for, and requires the support of many more people than the inventors and early adopters ever imagined.

Ask Ignaz Semmelweis, the Hungarian physician who, in 1847, observed that doctors performing autopsies were carrying "cadaverous particles" to their patients during childbirth, causing deadly infections.[53] When he implemented mandatory handwashing with chlorinated lime solution, maternal mortality rates plummeted dramatically. But the medical establishment was offended at the suggestion that gentlemen doctors could cause infections. They rejected his evidence, ridiculed his theories, and eventually had him committed to

53 Uvi Tyagi and Kailash Chander Barwal, "Ignac Semmelweis—Father of Hand Hygiene," *The Indian Journal of Surgery* vol. 82, 3 (2020): 276-277, doi:10.1007/s12262-020-02386-6.

an asylum, where he died from an infection—the very thing he had spent his life trying to prevent. Only years later, when Louis Pasteur's work on germ theory provided the scientific framework, did the medical community accept what Semmelweis had proven all along.

And rightly so, in a way. For thousands of years, healers have been trying to perfect how best to care for people, and it's always been "Do the best you can" with the latest tools and knowledge. Today, experimentation has been largely replaced by evidence-based practice and guidelines that prioritize patient safety.

And I recognize that building a system to care for one hundred million Americans in healthcare provider shortage areas across fifty states and three territories and nearly four million square miles with excellence is a process, not an event.

If you're working in mobile health today and feel like you're fighting an uphill battle against skeptical administrators, resistant payers, and entrenched systems, remember Semmelweis.

But the evidence is on your side. The outcomes speak for themselves. And while the resistance can be maddening, history shows that revolutionary healthcare innovations eventually prevail when they demonstrably improve patient outcomes. The work is worth it, even when it feels like you're standing alone against conventional wisdom. Pioneering leaders are often lonely.

Advancing Technology

A mother of three sits in her darkened kitchen at midnight, a coughing baby on her lap, a tablet with a cracked screen propped against a box of cereal. A doctor's face glows online. In twenty minutes, a telehealth visit delivers a diagnosis and a prescription from the corner drug store to pick up in the morning. No missing work, no hour-long drive, and no other babies coughing on her little ones in a germ-filled waiting room. Relief floods her.

This is the promise of telehealth.

That same night, a few streets away, her neighbor, an elderly widower, sits at his kitchen table and stares at his locked phone. He cannot recall the password for that app that schedules his diabetes check-ins. He's running low on glucose strips, his eyesight is a little blurry, and fatigue presses on his shoulders. After the third failed attempt, he tosses the phone on the table, lowers his head into his hands, and whispers, "Forget it." Hopelessness floods him.

Two houses, two people, one technology. One gains relief. One loses hope.

Digital health is no longer an approaching wave; it is the water we are swimming in. How we handle it has the potential to multiply the reach of good medicine or deepen the chasm of inequality.

Patients today measure every service by the speed of a tap and the certainty of a tracking number. Retail giants have taught us to expect movies on demand and packages delivered to our doorstep; we naturally expect healthcare to answer with the same convenience.

Many in medicine have responded with video visits, medication by mail, and digital dashboards that track every lab result. For the woman in the kitchen, those innovations feel like grace.

Yet, as we see in the case of the widower, caring for people cannot be fully reduced to bandwidth, battery life, and video calls.

Almost half of American households without reliable internet are Black or Hispanic. Rural counties struggle for basic connectivity. A brilliant app conceived in Silicon Valley will wither in Appalachia or the inner city, not through lack of goodwill but through simple absence of signal. Progress that lifts the affluent while leaving the vulnerable behind is not progress at all; it is camouflage for the status quo. Technology must eventually kneel before humanity: To succeed, it must work for both early adopters through to the risk-averse late majority.

Data carries the same dual edge. Hospitals now collect oceans of numbers—vital signs streamed from wearables, imaging files the size of novels, genetic blueprints that read like infinite barcodes. Properly harnessed, those rivers of information can predict heart failure from miles away before the first short breath or flag a lung malignancy long before a tumor casts shadows on a screen.

But information without context is just expensive clutter, and valuable context lives in places algorithms cannot see—untied shoes, stained pants, mold in a bathroom, an empty refrigerator, the palpable grief in a man or woman who simply stopped eating after the funeral of their lifelong love, which can only be felt while sitting knee to knee.

Eighty percent of what determines health happens outside a clinic, in the messy texture of daily life. The social determinants hiding in plain sight—food insecurity, housing instability, transportation barriers—are exactly what mobile health programs uncover and help address.

When a mobile clinic parks in a food desert, providers don't only see the diabetes; they see the corner store with no fresh produce, the bus route that doesn't connect to the grocery store, the reality that shapes every decision. Until technology learns to see that texture and protect the privacy of those who share it, data may sparkle, but it will not illuminate.

Telehealth has earned its applause for collapsing distance and making the most of our time. A cardiologist in Manhattan can now guide a farmer in Montana through medication adjustments. A single mother can slip into her parked car on a lunch break and speak with a pediatrician. These gains matter.

Still, anyone who has practiced medicine knows there are many blind spots on a screen. A camera cannot feel an abdomen that tightens beneath gentle pressure, or catch that faint fruity odor hinting at ketoacidosis, or notice the tremor revealed only when physician and patient shake hands.

Bodies are stubbornly analog. Some diseases whisper before they shout, and those whispers often travel through touch, smell, or the fleeting pallor of skin—signals too subtle for pixels.

This is where mobile health programs find their sweet spot, bringing both technology and human presence directly to communities. A mobile health program can offer the convenience of digital tools while preserving the irreplaceable value of physical examination and human connection. When providers can simultaneously access electronic health records, deploy point-of-care diagnostics, and lay healing hands on patients, they bridge the gap between digital efficiency and analog wisdom.

We also can't forget a central truth: Relationships are an integral part of every prescription. Study after study shows that a trusted bond between clinician and patient improves adherence, reduces readmission, and even lowers malpractice claims. When a physician listens without hurry, hope rises, cortisol falls, and choices bend toward health. No line of code can replace that human alchemy. We must use digital tools to buy us more minutes for human contact, not to reduce them.

The economics are equally complex. Health systems investing millions in digital infrastructure often see disappointing returns when their target populations can't or won't engage with the technology. Mobile health programs, by contrast, can achieve both digital efficiency and human connection—maximizing both patient outcomes and the quality bonuses that follow. When technology serves the mission rather than dominating it, ROI becomes measurable in both dollars and lives.

Leadership, like always, is the hinge on which the future swings. The question each healthcare leader must ask is brutally simple: Does this innovation solve a real problem for the people who need us most? If the answer is yes, deploy it with courage. If the answer is no—or not yet—refine it, simplify it, or set it aside.

Clinicians report feeling more connected to their purpose when they can combine digital efficiency with meaningful patient interaction—exactly what mobile health programs facilitate. When providers can spend less time wrestling with technology and more time engaging with patients, burnout decreases, and job satisfaction rises. The future of healthcare depends on innovations that energize rather than exhaust the people delivering care.

Design every digital path for the patient least equipped to travel it; everyone else will manage the journey just fine. Measure success not by downloads but by lower A1c and fewer asthma flares and by nights of sleep reclaimed from worry. Integrate new tools so seamlessly that clinicians feel lighter, not laden; otherwise, we are pouring water on a drowning swimmer.

The future of medicine is not a choice between silicon and stethoscope. It is a braided cord of virtual visits for routine care, remote sensors that call for help before danger peaks, and in-person encounters reserved for the mysteries only hands, eyes, and human presence can solve. Technology offers reach; touch offers depth. Patients deserve both.

We do not need perfect answers before we act. We need leaders willing to try, listen, measure, and try again, with the patient's dignity always at the center. When technology serves that mission, it becomes more than machinery; it becomes ministry. And that is how the promise overtakes the peril of technology.

A Blueprint for Mobile Health

Remember our two neighbors from a few pages back? The one video conferencing with her doctor and the other who gave up trying to log in to his app for a diabetes check-in? The solution isn't choosing between the two scenarios; it's creating a bridge that serves them both.

One bridge can be mobile health but not in the way most people think about it. We're not talking about sending a van with a nurse to check blood pressure at the county fair. We're talking about a fundamental reimagining of how healthcare reaches people, combining the best of both worlds our neighbors represent. We need a new model.

Before we talk about that model, we need to understand why it's needed. We've shown you already the sobering comparison—that a fire engine can get to nearly every house in America in less than ten minutes, but rural Americans travel an average of twenty-seven minutes each way for routine health visits.

Our research highlights six major reasons for this disparity, all directly or indirectly related to population density.

First, there's the economic reality: Smaller communities cannot absorb the expenses of a full-time medical practice and the associated providers. While there is always a gap in the market, there's not always a market in the gap.

Second, there's intensity: Rural firehouses are active only as needed, while traditional healthcare facilities are expected to be open normal business hours and fully staffed.

Third, payment methodology has reduced Medicaid fee-for-service reimbursements for clinical services to commodity levels, with a rate reflective of high-volume group practices. This payment structure doesn't differentiate for services delivered in sites more likely to serve high-risk patients. Current methodology does, by contrast, systematically incentivize health systems to trade population health for procedure volume.

Fourth, physician finances create an impossible situation. A volunteer firefighter can train at night and on weekends. A family physician spends over a decade learning their craft and shoulders large loans. Unlike firefighters supported by local governments, opening a practice in a sparsely populated area puts a physician at personal financial risk.

Fifth, workforce shortages compound the problem—in 2022, 7.8 percent of US counties didn't have an established practicing primary care physician.[54]

Sixth, there's what researchers call distance decay. What consumers believe about healthcare convenience is well studied. As McKinsey found, "Consumers look for care that is close to home."[55] Longer distance, time, and higher transportation costs impose "travel costs," which create a tax-like effect that lowers utilization of health services.[56] A convenient location is reported as a priority for about half of consumers.[57]

Even when scheduling telehealth appointments, two-thirds of telehealth appointments are booked within driving distance of home, potentially in anticipation of future in-person appointments.

---

54 National Center for Health Workforce Analysis, *State of the Primary Care Workforce, 2024* (Health Resources and Services Administration, 2024).

55 Jenny Buchter et al., "Consumers Rule: Driving Healthcare Growth with a Consumer-Led Strategy," *McKinsey & Company*, April 15, 2024.

56 Ibrahim Demir and M. Mahmud Khan, "Estimating the Effects of Travel Distance and Costs of Emergency Department (ED) Utilization: Learnings from Individual Level Data," *International Journal of Economics and Finance Studies* 9, no. 1 (2017): 64–76.

57 E. P. Mseke et al., "Distance and/or Travel Time Decay and Healthcare Access for Rural and Remote Residents in OECD Countries: A Scoping Review," *Journal of Transport & Health* 37, no. 101819 (2024).

Willingness to engage in healthcare consumption decays regularly in ten-mile increments of driving distance. Every mile matters, as does every minute and every barrier.

So instead of trying to put a brick-and-mortar clinic in every small town, the model we recommend leverages principles of distribution and logistics long recognized by food, fuel, and package delivery industries to resolve these conflicts and more efficiently distribute healthcare.

The genius of mobile health isn't just that it goes to patients but that it can synthesize population density in a way that makes healthcare delivery financially sustainable. Take a rural county with ten thousand people spread across one thousand square miles. A brick-and-mortar clinic needs patients to come to it and struggles with sparse population density. A mobile health program can visit five communities of two thousand people each, creating by movement a population density equivalent to a small city.

Mobile health also doesn't have to choose between high tech and high touch. The program becomes a technology platform that moves through communities, bringing both human presence and digital capabilities to where people live and work.

Picture this: a mobile clinic equipped with point-of-care diagnostics, telemedicine capabilities, and broadband internet. It parks in a rural community that has poor cell service. Suddenly, that community has access to specialists through telemedicine, immediate lab results, and electronic health records that connect to the regional health system. But here's the crucial part: It's still fundamentally about human relationships. The same provider returns to the same community regularly. Trust gets built. Health behaviors change. Quality metrics and outcomes improve. The technology enhances the relationship; it doesn't replace it.

When we build mobile health networks, we're not just creating healthcare delivery—we're creating healthcare resilience. Fixed infrastructure is brittle. Mobile infrastructure is antifragile.

When health disparities in a community change over time, mobile health can change with them. When one community's needs are met, resources can shift to where they're needed most.

When disasters strike, mobile health networks could possibly be a first responder and then support any long-term solutions. Brick-and-mortar healthcare access points and supply chains are stuck in one place, and often it's the wrong place to begin. Surging behavioral health, even more than medical, is critical to recovery in some cases.

Expanding primary care access in rural areas via this model is a high-leverage process improvement. Research predicts that combining improved geographic accessibility with process standardization will improve the quality and reliability of primary care delivery in rural areas.

The structural shift of reducing the distance between patients and primary care providers drives measurable cost savings. While a standardized network of satellite primary care clinics may not serve every patient, improve every metric, or capture every dollar of savings, it does enjoy a distinctive flexibility and is built to leverage the principles of continuous improvement.

The result is a quality improvement system that health plans and managed care organizations can leverage from one single point of control to boost at least six flagship quality metrics around access to care in rural communities, reducing ED utilization, controlling chronic conditions, and together bending the cost curve downward.

For healthcare leaders, this means thinking beyond the walls of your facilities. It means measuring success not just by patients served but by communities reached. It means building partnerships that allow mobile health to thrive with payers, with technology companies, with community organizations.

For policymakers, it means creating payment systems that reward mobile health for what it accomplishes: better health outcomes at lower cost. It means removing regulatory barriers that prevent mobile health from reaching its full potential. It means recognizing that mobile health isn't an add-on to the healthcare system; it's a fundamental part of how healthcare should work.

For communities, it means demanding better than the false choice between high tech and high touch. It means supporting mobile health initiatives that bring both to your doorstep. It means recognizing that healthcare equity doesn't happen by accident—it happens by design.

The future of healthcare is mobile, but not in the way most people think. It's not about apps and devices; it's about bringing the full power of modern healthcare to every community, wrapped in the human relationships that make healthcare work.

A County-by-County Infrastructure Plan

The challenge of delivering healthcare more efficiently isn't that we don't know where the gaps and disparities are. It is that we've never built a system dynamic enough to close them as the details emerge from the data.

Think about it: Every month, new data shows us exactly where access to care is declining. A rural hospital closes in southern Georgia. A specialist practice shuts down in eastern Montana. A federally qualified health center loses funding in West Virginia. We document these losses, study them, write papers about them. But we don't respond to them with system and method.

What if we could?

Picture Clay County, Kentucky. The data is telling a story that no one is listening to. ED visits are up 15 percent over the past six months. The local primary care clinic is overwhelmed. The nearest specialist is three hours away. People are driving themselves to the emergency room for things that should be handled in a doctor's office, but there isn't a doctor's office that can or will see them.

In the traditional healthcare system, this crisis will be documented, studied, and maybe addressed in three to five years through some combination of physician recruitment, facility construction, and funding negotiations. Meanwhile, people in Clay County will continue to suffer.

But imagine if we had built something different. Imagine if Clay County's deteriorating health access metrics triggered an immediate response. Not a study or a committee or a five-year plan, but the deployment of actual healthcare resources. In thirty days, community health coalitions are formed, and soon a mobile health unit rolls into Clay County, staffed and equipped to provide primary care. Patients are connected to specialists via telemedicine, and population health services are delivered to address the root causes of those ED visits.

This isn't theoretical. The technology exists. The ability exists.

Six months later, when Clay County's metrics improve, that mobile unit could redeploy to Pike County, where new data shows emerging gaps. The system would be constantly responding, constantly adapting, constantly working to prevent health equity gaps from becoming health equity crises.

This is what mobile health makes possible: a healthcare delivery system that's agile enough to go where it's needed most, when it's needed most. But it only works if we're measuring the right things and deploying the right tools.

Traditional healthcare metrics tell us what happened, not what's about to happen. We need predictive indicators that let us intervene before gaps become crises. Some counties signal distress through healthcare utilization patterns—increasing ED visits, rising readmission rates, declining preventive care. Others signal through social determinants—rising unemployment, declining educational attainment, increasing poverty rates. Still others signal through infrastructure—broadband access declining, transportation options disappearing, retail pharmacies closing.

The key is building an intelligence system that can synthesize signals into actionable insights. When multiple indicators in a county start trending negatively, mobile health resources deploy. When a county's indicators improve, resources redeploy to where they're needed most.

But not every county needs the same intervention. Some need primary care access. Others need specialty care. Some need social services integration. Others need mental health support. The system needs to be smart enough to match the intervention to the specific gap.

This is where the county-by-county approach becomes powerful. Instead of one-size-fits-all solutions, the system can deploy customized interventions based on each county's specific needs and characteristics. Urban counties might need different approaches than rural ones. Counties with aging populations might need different services than counties with young families.

A national network of mobile health programs becomes the delivery mechanism for these customized interventions. One unit might be configured as a primary care clinic. Another as a specialty care hub. A third as a mental health center. The same physical infrastructure but reconfigured based on what each county needs.

The beauty of this approach is that it learns from itself. Every intervention generates data about what works and what doesn't. Every deployment teaches the system something new about how to respond to health equity gaps. Over time, the system becomes more sophisticated in its predictions and more effective in its interventions. It learns which early warning signs are most predictive of health access decline. It learns which interventions are most effective for which types of communities. It learns how to prevent health equity gaps before they emerge.

This approach sidesteps many of the political challenges that have stymied healthcare reform. It doesn't require massive federal legislation or state-by-state implementation. It doesn't pit rural against urban or red states against blue states. It's simply a systematic approach to deploying existing resources where they can do the most good. Counties that don't need intervention aren't penalized. Counties that do need intervention aren't stigmatized. The system simply responds to data with resources, targeting intervention where it's needed most.

The biggest challenge to scaling this system isn't technical—it's operational. Building a mobile health response network capable of serving more than three thousand counties requires a lot of coordination. It requires standardized equipment, shared protocols, integrated data systems, and seamless logistics. But the payoff is enormous. Instead of reactive healthcare delivery that responds to crises after they've become entrenched, we could have proactive healthcare delivery that prevents crises before they emerge. Instead of documenting health equity gaps, we could be closing them.

Picture America in 2030: No county experiences prolonged health access decline because mobile health response networks intervene before gaps become crises. Health equity isn't an aspiration—it's an operational reality maintained through continuous monitoring and targeted intervention.

This isn't utopian thinking. It's systems thinking applied to healthcare equity. It's recognizing that mobile health's greatest strength isn't just that it can go anywhere—it's that it can go where it's needed most, when it's needed most.

Chapter 16

Healing the Healers

There's a moment in every home renovation show when the sledgehammer comes out. The homeowners take that first swing at the wall separating their kitchen from the dining room. Dust flies, chunks of drywall crash to the floor, and suddenly there's light streaming through where a barrier used to be. The family can finally talk to each other while dinner is being cooked.

When I consider the pioneers of mobile health highlighted in this book, that's how I see them. They are breaking down walls. But the walls these programs crush not only help patients but also free the healers. The other wall that desperately needs to come down is the one between doctors and their inherent passion for caring for people.

David Vliet learned this during his final negotiation as CEO of LifeLong Medical Care in Northern California. The doctors made an unusual request: They wanted to shift their patient-facing time from 80 percent to 60 percent so they could spend the other 40 percent thinking about their cases.

Think about that. Highly trained scientists asking for more time to think.

"What I believe is that we should be introducing mobile health modalities to healthcare providers because, to the extent that while these brilliant humans are sitting in the office grinding through twenty-two or twenty-three patients a day, we are literally losing them," Vliet said. "It's extremely hard to retain providers over time ..."

Providers want to become more than patient-processing machines in windowless exam rooms. They want to interact with patients on a deeper level. To put it simply: When you spend most of your working day in rooms with no windows, it's nice to see the sun occasionally.

Vliet has spent over three decades as an executive in the federally qualified health center world, working in Florida, Texas, California, and Latin America. He's negotiated fees for services, worked with local governmental agencies, negotiated union contracts. He understands the totality of the economic picture. What he's learned is that we're grinding doctors into dust.

"That's so true when you put it in those terms," Vliet said. "We, as a society, have not reinvented the work. These providers are being ground into dust because, at least when I ran a health center, my profit-and-loss margin was what kept it going. The margin, that counter that had to be a certain number of patients per provider, that's what I had to make sure we had an adequate margin by the end of the year. It does not take into consideration how hard the work is or how complex the patients are. It doesn't take into consideration that we are taking highly trained scientists who really shouldn't be treated as robots but really are because we have to keep up the volume."

About 65 percent of rural areas have a shortage of primary care physicians. But the real crisis isn't just numbers—it's what we're doing to the doctors we have.

That's where Vliet sees mobile health as vital not only for treating patients but also for reinvigorating doctors who need to see the sun a little more often.

"My theory is that people, in general, and doctors, specifically, want to get out and do something meaningful. If we can get them out of the grind and maybe reduce the cost structure and put them in an environment where they can be more creative and have a scene change, maybe take care of a variety of patients, that's where mobile can really be helpful," Vliet said.

He's seen this firsthand. Vliet worked with several doctors who practiced "street medicine," where clinicians literally leave their offices behind to go out and find patients on the street, help them, examine them, and try to improve their lives.

For them, it was fascinating work. Extremely difficult, but fascinating and cool. It was an adventure to find unique cases on the street. It was enthralling to meet people and improve their lives. It was, in its own way, the picture of why people get into healthcare. The draw like no other.

"They want the stuff that's sexy, that's cool. That's the stuff that gets them excited. They love that stuff, even though it's really hard, because it's groovy and it's God's work," Vliet said.

What mobile health can do is bring back some of that. It may not be every day or even more than once a week or once every two weeks. But it's there, and it's important to energize the mindset of so many doctors who are caught up in crunching numbers to support a clinic.

The most meaningful time of Vliet's professional career happened during COVID-19. As the pandemic unfolded, he, several doctors, and many others from LifeLong had to hit the streets. They literally rang doorbells, dressed in masks and hospital garb, searching for anyone they could help with tests or vaccines.

"It was truly one of the best times for us from a feeling of satisfaction and value," Vliet said. "We were out there, connecting with the community, knocking on doors, trying to do the best we could to really just help people."

At his core, that's what Vliet always wanted to do. When he entered community healthcare, it was still dominated by direct descendants of the Jack Geiger prototype—doctors and healthcare workers trying to save every individual.

"The OGs of the Civil Rights movement era of community healthcare really tried to get into the nooks and crannies of health issues," Vliet said. "I was happy to be around for that golden era where we had a lot of smart people in the movement who embraced larger-scale issues while understanding where this all started."

The overarching philosophy for anyone in healthcare is to do work that directly serves a patient and has a wonderful outcome. Say as much as you want about big ideas and alternative modalities, but the real satisfaction comes from solving a problem or saving a life. It comes from finding people who desperately need you and trying to solve their problem. And if you're searching for those types of people, the best way to find them is to work in a mobile health program.

"I know the work we did created ripples across the community that you couldn't see," Vliet said. "We all knew it, and we took incredible satisfaction from it. If we avoided an emergency visit or got better glasses for someone or got a better smile for a child or got someone's diabetes managed, that had a direct effect on their lives. It also impacted the community and lowered the cost for taking care of those people."

The mobile health model offers providers meaningful work through patient-centered, community-based care without sacrificing compensation or career trajectory. It provides flexibility for providers to reside and raise families in population centers while serving outlying communities. It offers intellectually challenging problems that multiply their impact from individuals to communities, with agency to make the right calls and freedom to innovate, iterate, and lead.

Most healthcare jobs force talented people to spend time on routine cases that don't fully utilize their education, expertise, or experience. The most joyful, engaged, productive healthcare workers feel both physically and psychologically safe, perceive belonging, appreciate the meaning and purpose of their work, have choice and control over their time, experience camaraderie, and perceive their work life to be fair and equitable.

Mobile health provides all those components.

We're talking about putting the joy back into healthcare and reinvigorating that desire people had when they first wanted to become doctors. There was once joy in hearing someone say, "The doctor is here," and then for that doctor to snap his bag shut after a successful visit. What was once good can be good again.

"You see it with so many doctors; they just have their head down, and they're going and going and going, plowing through one appointment after another and not taking time to really think about what they are trying to accomplish," Vliet said.

That's a bleak existence for people who have hopes and dreams of achieving something bigger with their professional lives. When mobility is integrated into healthcare, the future of the industry can be something filled with joy and promise, not just another day of clocking eight hours of appointments and then taking notes home to finish.

Success in reducing health disparities creates clear career progression opportunities as providers take on responsibility for adjacent communities, networks, states, and national roles. The work grows with the worker. It's meaningful work in the deepest sense—work that connects providers to their highest calling, that lets them be healers in the fullest meaning of that word. It's work that's groovy and cool and challenging and, as Vliet says, God's work.

A Culture Transformation

Dr. Coley King has been practicing street medicine for years, but he'll never forget the day Venice Family Clinic's mobile unit arrived at the peak of COVID-19's most lethal surge in Los Angeles County.

"Homeless people were having much more difficulty getting into medical buildings, transportation was limited, and they were in a mentality of being sheltered in one place to avoid getting the disease," Dr. King said. "That was an important time to deliver healthcare services to people where they are. We were able to help people out when traditional healthcare systems were struggling to meet their needs."

But something unexpected happened. The mobile clinic didn't just transform care for homeless patients—it transformed the entire organization's sense of purpose.

"It was an expensive idea, and we didn't have anyone to copy," said Dr. King, the clinic's director of homeless health. "I was nervous how it would turn out."

The experiment proved successful, he said, and helped change not just the methods of street medicine in Los Angeles County but the culture of Venice Family Clinic itself.

"I have been able to see more patients since we got the van," said Dr. King. "More importantly, the quality of healthcare that we have been able to deliver is much higher. We can bring vaccines; we are able to do lab testing and extensive wound care. And if patients wish, we can offer them more privacy. It's a well-stocked, beautiful modern space."

That's the hidden power of mobile health programs: They don't just impact the communities they serve or the providers who staff them. They transform the culture of the entire organization.

Healthcare executives have been struggling with organizational culture for years. Employee engagement surveys show declining satisfaction. Staff turnover is at historic highs. The phrase *moral injury* has become commonplace in healthcare leadership circles. People who went into healthcare to help others often feel disconnected from that mission, buried under administrative tasks and corporate metrics.

Mobile health programs cut through all that noise. They create tangible, visible evidence that the organization is fulfilling its mission. They give every employee—from the C-suite to the cafeteria—connection to people and stories they can tell with pride about the work their organization does.

The numbers from healthcare worker studies back this up. Research shows that healthcare workers find the most satisfaction in a sense of dedication and in feeling that they are a vital resource to others. Nurses in intensive care settings, for instance, have described their work not as simply helping people but as the privilege of being present with others through the most profound moments of life — and of offering hope in the midst of those experiences.[58]

Mobile health programs provide exactly this kind of meaningful work. They offer healthcare workers the chance to be "where things are happening" on the front lines and serve as a source for communities that have been left behind.

58 Dip Raj Thapa et al., "Tasks Contributing to Job Satisfaction Among Health Professionals: A Qualitative Descriptive Study," *Nursing Open* 12, no. 10 (2025): e70338, https://doi.org/10.1002/nop2.70338.

At Saban Community Clinic in Los Angeles, physician assistant Samantha Kumpf sees this transformation firsthand. Working in the clinic's mobile unit serving homeless populations, she's witnessed how different the work feels compared to traditional healthcare settings.

"They can get judged for how they dress or for their substance use," she said about how homeless patients are often treated in hospitals. "It discourages homeless people from visiting emergency rooms."

But in the mobile clinic, Kumpf described building real relationships with patients over time. "We build relationships with the people we treat. It helps with follow-ups, considering that patients need recurring examinations."

Robert Stennis, a forty-five-year-old homeless patient who has been seeing Saban's mobile team for about a year, captured the difference: "They know my medical history. They interact with me. It feels like they are on my team."

"We are on your team," Kumpf echoed during his visit—a moment that illustrates why healthcare workers are drawn to mobile health programs. It's medicine as relationship, not just transaction.

The cultural impact extends far beyond the mobile unit staff. Organizations with mobile health programs report higher employee satisfaction scores, lower turnover rates, and improved physician recruitment. But the real impact is harder to measure—it's the pride employees feel when they can point to something their organization does that's unambiguously good.

Healthcare workers consistently report that their greatest source of professional pride comes from two things: the quality of care they provide to patients and families, and the caliber of the teams they work alongside. Mobile health programs deliver on both fronts. They offer tangible evidence of meaningful care reaching vulnerable populations, and they build tight-knit teams whose members develop the kind of adaptability and clinical range that comes from working outside the walls of a traditional facility. For many healthcare workers, that combination — doing excellent work with excellent people, often with limited resources — is precisely what makes the work worth doing.[59]

Mobile health programs give healthcare workers that same sense of pride—the feeling that they're part of something meaningful, that they're taking on challenges and making a difference despite resource constraints.

The recruitment advantages are significant. In a tight labor market, organizations with mobile programs have a differentiator. They can tell prospective employees a story about community impact that goes beyond typical healthcare marketing. They can show, not just tell, that the organization is committed to serving the underserved.

The retention benefits are equally important. Healthcare workers are leaving the profession at unprecedented rates, citing burnout, moral distress, and disconnection from the mission. Mobile health programs provide a counternarrative—they remind people why healthcare work matters.

Research shows that healthcare workers derive their greatest satisfaction from a sense of dedication to their work and from the privilege of being present with people during their most vulnerable moments. They find meaning not just in clinical outcomes but in the human connection that caregiving demands.

Mobile health programs offer all of this. They position healthcare workers as vital community resources, providing care to people in truly vulnerable circumstances, making a tangible difference in society.

---

59 Les Masterson, "Pride a Key Factor in Healthcare Employee Satisfaction: LinkedIn Survey," *Healthcare Dive*, June 27, 2018, https://www.healthcaredive.com/news/pride-a-key-factor-in-healthcare-employee-satisfaction-linkedin-survey/526634/.

But perhaps the most important cultural impact is on organizational identity. Healthcare executives are under enormous pressure to balance financial performance with mission fulfillment. Mobile health programs can do both; they can be financially sustainable while also creating the kind of community impact that healthcare leaders went into healthcare to achieve.

Dr. King's reflection on Venice Family Clinic's mobile program captures this perfectly: "We were able to help people out when traditional healthcare systems were struggling to meet their needs."

That's the promise of mobile health for healthcare executives: not just better community health outcomes but better organizational health outcomes. A culture that's aligned with healthcare's highest calling, employees who are proud of the work they do, and an organization that embodies its mission in a way that's visible, tangible, and transformative.

The culture transformation isn't automatic. It requires intentional communication, story sharing, and integration with the organization's broader mission. But when it works, it gives healthcare workers something they rarely find in traditional settings — the sense that they are part of something larger, walking alongside patients and communities through moments that matter. That's exactly the kind of meaningful work that drew them to healthcare in the first place.

In an era when healthcare organizations are struggling with culture, engagement, and purpose, mobile health programs offer something increasingly rare: a way to do well by doing good. They prove that serving the underserved isn't just morally right—it's organizationally transformative.

Beyond Healthcare: The Mobile Clinic Has a Hitch

When The Family Van began parking in Boston neighborhoods in 1992, Dr. Nancy Oriol and her team thought they were simply providing health screenings. They were wrong.

A recent study on the causes for delays in treatment after the first signs of stroke found that 75 percent of African Americans called a friend or relative first, and only 12 percent called 911 first. This inclination to reach out to a trusted friend when in medical need was the basis for the creation of the Knowledgeable Neighbor model.[60]

The Family Van's Knowledgeable Neighbor approach was designed to make healthcare providers trusted friends in the community. But something unexpected happened over the years. The mobile clinic didn't just become a trusted member of the community; it became the community's go-to advisor on everything that affected people's lives.

One of the most common misconceptions about mobile health is that simply showing up is enough — that parking a vehicle in an underserved neighborhood will automatically draw people in. The reality is more complicated. Communities that have been historically neglected by the healthcare system don't immediately trust an unfamiliar clinic on wheels. Building that trust takes time, consistency, and a willingness to overcome the skepticism that comes from years of being overlooked.

But the Family Van team understood something profound: When you show up consistently with competent, compassionate care, you become more than a healthcare provider. You become a community

60 Caterina Hill et al., "Knowledgeable Neighbors: A Mobile Clinic Model for Disease Prevention and Screening in Underserved Communities," *American Journal of Public Health* 102, no. 3 (2012): e12–e18.

resource that people trust not just with their bodies but with their questions, their fears, their hopes for something better.

The progression was predictable. First, The Family Van established credibility through excellent medical care. By 2012, the program's database contained data from more than eighty thousand patient visits, predominantly serving minorities—62 percent Black, 23 percent Hispanic, 21 percent White.[61,62] Of those screened, 60 percent had previously undetected elevated blood pressure, 14 percent had previously undetected elevated blood glucose, and 38 percent had previously undetected elevated total cholesterol.[63]

But the real breakthrough came when the healthcare team realized they weren't just treating medical conditions—they were treating the social determinants that created those conditions. The trust built through medical care opened a channel for addressing the root causes of health disparities.

Mobile health programs create a platform for addressing those social determinants that drive the medical needs in the first place. Compassionate care is just the first step to developing trust and influence in a community. Once that channel is open, it paves the way to shared values, literacy, governance, housing, and a myriad of social determinants of health.

This progression from service to influence to empowerment isn't unique to The Family Van. It's a pattern that emerges wherever mobile health programs are allowed to develop deep community relationships.

---

61 Zirui Song et al., "Mobile Clinic in Massachusetts Associated with Cost Savings from Lowering Blood Pressure and Emergency Department Use," *Health Affairs* 32, no. 1 (2013): 36–44.

62 Zoe Bouchelle et al., "Preventive Care for Patients in Mobile Clinics: Results from a Survey at The Family Van," *International Journal for Equity in Health* 16, no. 1 (2017).

63 Meri Aung et al., "The Emerging Business Models and Value Proposition of Mobile Health Clinics," *American Journal of Accountable Care* 5, no. 4 (2017): 38–42.

Research shows that mobile health clinics "often address important social determinants of health including food and housing insecurity, education, and job opportunities." They succeed because they "address both medical and social determinants of health, tackling health issues on a population level by working with communities to build capacity and promote health."[64]

Consider how this plays out in practice. A mobile health clinic serving migrant farmworkers in California's Central Valley began with basic medical care for work-related injuries and illnesses. But as trust developed, the healthcare providers learned about the living and working conditions that were driving many of the health problems they were treating.

The providers discovered that they were treating respiratory infections, but the workers were living in overcrowded housing with poor ventilation. They were treating heat exhaustion, but the workers had no access to shade or adequate water breaks.

The mobile team began documenting these conditions and advocating for change. They partnered with labor organizations to improve workplace safety standards. They connected with housing organizations to address living conditions. They worked with legal aid societies to help workers understand their rights. The medical care gave them credibility, but the relationships gave them influence.

Similarly, research on mobile health documents how they "build trust with underserved populations" by "being able to go to them, make the effort to get right where they are—say here I am. I'm here

64 Nelson C. Malone et al., "Mobile Health Clinics in the United States," *International Journal for Equity in Health* 19, no. 40 (2020): 1–9, https://equityhealthj.biomedcentral.com/articles/10.1186/s12939-020-1135-7.

to respond to you. It's a good way to be able to bring them into a healthcare system that maybe they are distrustful of."[65]

This trust becomes the foundation for broader community transformation. The mobile program's documentation of health problems related to social determinants contributes to policy changes. Its advocacy helps secure funding for community improvements. Its partnerships with educational organizations help families succeed. It moves from treating symptoms to addressing causes.

The Family Van model demonstrates this perfectly. Its Knowledgeable Neighbor approach incorporates several key strategies:

- Community health workers who are often from the communities they serve
- Cultural competence training for staff
- Long-term weekly presence in neighborhoods (established since 1992)
- Strong collaborations with community health centers, hospitals, churches, and others
- Patient-centered care that puts clients in control of their health decisions

"Mobile has flipped healthcare on its head, and we provide care at the convenience of the patient," explained one mobile health leader. "The providers allow themselves to become more personally connected and knowledgeable about people's lives and know their stories."[66]

---

65 Stephanie W. Y. Yu et al., "The Scope and Impact of Mobile Health Clinics in the United States: A Literature Review," *International Journal for Equity in Health* 16, no. 178 (2017), https://pmc.ncbi.nlm.nih.gov/articles/PMC5629787/.

66 Mobile Health Map, *The Case for Mobile* (Harvard Medical School, 2022), https://www.mobilehealthmap.org/wp-content/uploads/2022/11/The-Case-For-Mobile-2022-Updated.pdf.

This personal connection creates influence. When mobile health providers start talking about housing, education, or employment, people listen because they've demonstrated their commitment to the community. When they advocate for better services, their voice carries weight because they've established trust through consistent, quality care.

The influence extends beyond individual patient care to system-level change. Mobile health programs become catalysts for addressing the social determinants that create health disparities in the first place. They don't just treat disease—they build the capacity for communities to address the conditions that create disease.

This is the ultimate promise of mobile health programs: They create a platform for addressing health disparities at their source. The medical care establishes trust and credibility. The relationships create influence and voice. The influence enables system-level change that improves health outcomes for entire communities.

The progression follows a predictable pattern. First, the mobile clinic provides excellent medical care that meets an immediate need. Second, as trust deepens, community members begin sharing their broader challenges and looking to the healthcare providers for guidance beyond medical issues. Third, the healthcare providers use their influence to address the social determinants that drive health disparities. Finally, the community itself becomes empowered to advocate for change.

When you serve, you develop influence. When you have influence in a community, you can change beliefs. When you change beliefs, you drive behaviors. When you drive behaviors, you create systems. When you create systems, you generate results that help people at scale.

The mobile clinic has a hitch, and what can pull behind it is nothing less than the transformation of entire communities. The medical program is the platform, but community empowerment is the payload. That's how we can move from treating individual patients to improving population health. That's how we can move from managing disease to creating health.

That's the hitch. That's the power. And that's the promise of mobile health.

Conclusion

This Could Change the World

You've come a long way.

When you picked up this book, you might have known a lot or a little about mobile health. Perhaps you saw it as a nice idea that couldn't scale or an expensive solution to problems that already had answers. Maybe you were curious but cautious, wondering if this was just another healthcare fad that would fade when the next crisis hit.

But you stayed with the story. You walked alongside David Vliet as he found his way back to the heart of medicine. You witnessed communities transform when healthcare showed up where people lived, worked, and gathered. You saw the numbers that prove mobile health isn't just compassionate—it's effective, efficient, and sustainable.

Now you know something that most healthcare leaders don't know yet: We've been thinking about this wrong.

We've been trying to fix healthcare by making it more efficient, more digital, more centralized. We've been pouring resources into buildings and technology, assuming if we just make the system smart enough and fast enough, people will find their way to it. We've been treating symptoms while ignoring the disease.

But you now understand what transformational leaders across the country are beginning to discover: The solution isn't about perfecting a system we have but perhaps simply reimagining what healthcare might become.

We've engaged with some of these transformational leaders throughout this book: Dr. Coley King, taking Venice Family Clinic's mobile unit to homeless encampments during the worst of the pandemic. The team at The Family Van, building trust in Boston neighborhoods for over thirty years. The rural physicians who've discovered that mobile health lets them practice medicine the way they always dreamed. The healthcare executives who've watched their organizational cultures transform when their teams started doing work that they could be proud of.

These leaders have found a solution that works, and the reality is they are beginning to turn the tide. We see the number of mobile health programs reported by HRSA increasing exponentially year over year.

We've learned that today's healthcare ecosystem is well-intentioned but has a critical gap. The current model assumes that healthcare is a product to be delivered efficiently to consumers who will travel to receive it. It bets on the idea that making healthcare mildly inconvenient is OK because that will control utilization. It assumes that bigger is better, that centralization creates quality, that technology can substitute for relationship. These assumptions aren't evil, but they are wrong.

Healthcare isn't a product. It's not a service you receive. It's a partnership you enter with people you trust. It's not about the efficiency of the workflows. It is about the efficacy of the results. It's not about getting people to come to healthcare. It's about bringing healthcare to people.

You know this now. You've seen the evidence. You've heard the stories. You understand that mobile health isn't just an alternative delivery method but is a different way of thinking about what healthcare should be.

This will change the world. Or if not the entire world, at least someone's world.

How many worlds or lives it changes depends on how well it's done and how many people like you choose to act on what they learn, when they learn it.

Done poorly, mobile health looks like a niche solution for underserved populations—important but limited by financial sustainability. It's still important; done well for one person, it transforms a life. But done well for communities, it changes population health. Done well for organizations, it reshapes healthcare culture. Done well for our country, it redefines what our healthcare system can accomplish.

Done well for us all, it could usher in a new era of health and healing that our children will inherit.

I believe we are on the cusp of rediscovering one of our greatest strengths as a nation: the power of servant leadership. I see a new willingness to go where people are instead of demanding they come to us. Today, I feel a rising compassion to meet people in their circumstances instead of judging them for their choices. I detect a shift in speed and flexibility to adapting solutions to communities instead of forcing communities to adapt to solutions.

These have always been American values. The commandment to "Love thy neighbor as yourself" isn't just about caring for others; it's about caring for the people in your community with the same urgency you'd want for yourself and the same I would have wanted for my dad.

These are the values that built rural hospitals and urban clinics, that created the public health system and the safety net. They're the values that sent doctors to rural communities and nurses to urban neighborhoods. They're the values that made American healthcare the envy of the world before we lost our way in the maze of bureaucracy and profit.

Mobile health is about remembering that the point of any system is to serve people, not the other way around. It's about choosing relationship over transaction, compassion over efficiency, service over profit.

The choice is now yours.

You have the knowledge. You've seen the evidence. You understand the opportunity. You know that mobile health works—clinically, financially, and culturally. You know that it can transform individual lives, organizational cultures, and community health outcomes. You know that it addresses the workforce crisis, the access crisis, and the trust crisis that are plaguing healthcare today.

Now, while you were reading this book, something might have tugged a bit at your backbone, or made your heart pound a little, and a voice inside you might have said, "You can do this." When someone with character sees something wrong in the world, they are convicted and compelled to act and help right the wrong.

However, when the act required is big or comes with the danger of standing up and standing out, an innate subconscious fear of failure, reprisal, or the unknown will often rise to block that action and keep us safe. For this reason, people who make change need courage.

Without people of character and courage, our society will never do anything different from what we've always done and never get anything better than what we've always gotten. It takes people of character and courage to make things better in the world.

I'll warn you: Righting a wrong doesn't happen without opposition from incumbent players and ideas they threaten to displace. In what feels like the world's most welcoming field, I was surprised and disappointed by the viciousness and depth of the vitriol I encountered when I didn't bow to existing power structures and called out bad behavior in this space.

But that won't stop me or my team. I know that people often want to avoid accountability for their actions. And that everything worthwhile is uphill. But the view from the top is worth the climb.

The healthcare leaders we've met in this book—Dr. Nancy Oriol, Jerry Isikoff, Dr. Daniella Jaimes-Colina, Dr. Coley King, The Family Van team, David Vliet, and more—they each had to overcome that fear. They choose courage over comfort, action over inaction, change over the status quo.

Now it's your turn.

You also know that transformation doesn't happen automatically. Learning without application is of no value. Good things happen only when people like you decide to act on what they learn. Great things happen when leaders choose to lead, when innovators choose to innovate, when servants choose to serve and never give up.

Even when the opposition comes. Even when the entrenched interests fight back. Even when you're vilified for challenging the status quo.

If you're a healthcare provider, you can choose to explore mobile health to rediscover the joy and purpose that brought you to medicine in the first place. If you're a healthcare executive, you can choose to invest in mobile health to fulfill your mission while building a sustainable business. If you're a policymaker, you can choose to support mobile health to address health disparities while controlling costs. If you're a community leader, you can choose to advocate for mobile health to bring quality healthcare to your neighbors.

The choice is yours because the story is yours. You're not only the audience for this transformation. You're the hero.

Postscript

Our Team Is Changing the World

I'm about to tell you something personal that might surprise you. After everything you've read in this book—the mobile health programs, the mission, the fight for healthcare access—my real motivation isn't what you think it is.

But before I get to that, I want to share something that could change how you think about building teams and growing businesses. Buried in our story is a formula that took us from zero to $100 million in revenue in less than five years, with a team that actually looks forward to Monday mornings.

See, my father's death, that first mobile program, the nurse who hugged me, getting fired, starting over during COVID-19—all of that was just the setup. The real story is what I discovered about myself in the process and what that discovery taught me about unlocking potential in other people.

My family has always been lucky. We call ourselves "the Lucky LeFevers." It's not because everything goes our way but because whatever happens to us somehow turns out for the best. Take me for instance: Getting fired? That forced me to start this company. COVID-19 hitting right when we launched showed us exactly how desperate the world was for mobile healthcare. My dad dying broke my heart, but it opened my eyes to what really mattered to him.

Amanda saw this before I did. She's the steady one, the planner, the one who turns my wild ideas into actual systems. Every weekend for five years, she's been doing accounting and planning while I'm out talking to clients or working in the shop. She complements every one of my weaknesses and amplifies all my strengths. Without her, none of this works out.

When we started, we were complete outsiders in healthcare. We didn't know the acronyms, didn't understand the payment systems, didn't know who the players were. We got talked down to and frozen out of conferences, but, hey, you can't be mad at a dog for barking. But we had one thing going for us: We weren't afraid to work, and we were willing to learn.

And what we learned over the past five years has been eye-opening. Not just about healthcare but about what it really takes to build a team that thrives and an organization that makes a big difference in the world. And by the time I tell you what really drives me—and share the operating systems that made it all possible—you'll understand why this isn't just a business story. It's a blueprint for multiplying leaders and impact.

Here's one big thing we learned:

When we first got into mobile health, we thought the problem was simple: Health systems needed better, cheaper equipment. "If they only had better suppliers," we said, "they'd jump into this work."

So, we hired people and built systems to manufacture mobile clinics that were half the cost, delivered in half the time, with half the lifetime maintenance costs of anything else in the market.

Then we went to health systems and health centers with our equipment and asked them, "Ready to expand access to care now?"

"Well," they said, "these mobile units are just so hard to maintain. All those oil changes, tire rotations, inspections …"

OK. We went away and hired a team of mobile repair technicians and built a national network of service technicians. On-site maintenance, no downtime, full service. Problem solved.

Back to the health systems: "Now you want to do it, right?"

"The thing is," they said, "people tell us mobile programs are really complex. All the community partnerships, workflow design, procedure manuals …"

OK. We went away and hired implementation specialists. Our new team was full of folks who had successfully launched and optimized mobile health programs. We set them up to walk alongside our clients and make failure impossible.

Back to the health systems: "How about now?"

"Staffing is impossible. We can't find drivers, can't spare providers, don't have enough nurses …"

OK. We went away and built a staffing company. Healthcare recruiters, program managers, operations executives. We started running programs for clients who couldn't hire staff themselves.

"Surely now?"

"It's the money. The economics don't work. These programs lose money."

That's when I realized I'd had our ladder propped against the wrong wall for five years. These weren't operational problems—they were symptoms of something deeper. Health systems weren't failing to launch mobile programs because they couldn't figure out logistics. They were failing because they didn't have a financial model that made it worth their time.

I made a financial model with fully loaded costs and net benefits with allowances for different payer mixes and went on the road. I spoke at ten conferences, offering to partner with these health systems, providing equipment at no cost, with a model that produced hundreds of thousands of dollars a year in revenue in excess of costs. This generated some conversation because, as it turns out, most health systems were planning for four to five visits a day, staffing programs like they were big hospitals, and in many cases, they had no intention of billing for services at all.

Now we're getting under the hood—there was no single source of truth for this work to teach people. There was no institute or industry group, no accepted association, and no one to trust when it came to planning and evaluating the risks of these programs.

We started bringing pragmatic leaders in the space together to talk about it. We formed advisory councils. And as we gained momentum, we discovered we weren't just solving problems—we were building infrastructure for an entirely new way of delivering healthcare.

Every time someone said, "That's too hard," we said, "We'll make it easy." Every time they said, "We can't afford it," we said, "We'll make it profitable." Every time they said, "We don't know how," we said, "We'll show you."

But here's what really opened my eyes: The breakthrough I saw wasn't the systems we built or the financial models we created. It was watching the people around me grow into roles they'd never imagined they could fill. It was seeing them embrace the challenge of helping others and engaging in the work at a level I'd never seen or heard of before.

Because at the end of the day, you can have the best solutions to the world's problems in your pocket, but if you don't have people who believe in the mission and are willing to grow with you, you don't have anything of value.

That's when I realized what really gets me up every morning.

It wasn't the forty-six million Americans who need healthcare, the financial models, or even the vision of delivering healthcare to every corner of the country. It was watching Jan Rock transform from someone who was supposed to stay a few weeks into our chief people officer. It was seeing Neil Rotroff evolve from an industrial designer into a healthcare marketing expert. It was witnessing Brad Watson grow from a business development guy into a strategic partner who could sit knee to knee with health plan CEOs and have deep conversations about what they believe about quality and what their members need in the community.

What gets me up every morning is developing people. Finding people who are willing to grow beyond what they thought possible and then giving them everything they need to succeed.

Because my mentor John taught me that when you multiply leaders, you multiply impact far beyond what any one person could ever accomplish alone.

He said it's easy to be successful for yourself but much harder to be significant in the lives of others. That is servant leadership, in a nutshell, and it became my mission as a leader to take care of people in my charge and help them reach their full personal, professional, and financial potential.

This isn't just philosophy—it's how we operate. We built our entire foundation on proven leadership and business methodologies, but we don't use them like textbooks. We use them like instruction manuals. John Maxwell's book *25 Ways to Win with People* gives our team foundational people skills; then his *The 5 Levels of Leadership* guides us through development: from position (you have a job) to permission (people want to work with you) to production (you get results) to people development (you grow others) and finally to pinnacle (you multiply leaders).

Playing *The Great Game of Business* leverages my friend Jack Stack's forty years of open-book management experience, helping every one of our team members see exactly how the business is doing, where we're headed, and how their work contributes to the bigger picture. *The One-Hour Strategy* helps us decide what to do, and *The 4 Disciplines of Execution* keeps us focused as we do it. *Crossing the Chasm* helps us enter new markets with clockwork precision. These aren't motivational posters—they're operating systems in which we plant people with high potential. A place and a space where they can grow into the leaders they're meant to be. A place where love and accountability can grow together.

That goes for our clients and business partners as well. I love meeting people who arrive in our spaces thinking they are going to learn about mobile health but leave with their hearts marked with how we hold the principles of servant leadership and a newfound respect for their role as leaders in their organizations and their communities. Or executives who come in for business meetings but leave asking, "How did you create this culture? I wish our meetings were like this!"

I'll paint you a picture of what that looks like in practice.

Take Donnie Wingo, our director of manufacturing. Donnie symbolizes the heart of our business—we'll take care of it. Wingo was born and raised in Mooresville, North Carolina, a little more than an hour from Greensboro. For forty-two years, he worked in NASCAR. At age eighteen, he got a job as a team mechanic and worked his way up to becoming one of the best crew chiefs in the history of the sport. He has seven career NASCAR Cup victories to his name. He worked with drivers such as Jimmy Means, Morgan Shepherd, Geoff Bodine, Todd Bodine, Lake Speed, Dick Trickle, and Juan Pablo Montoya. He has a Daytona 500 trophy on his mantel.

For nearly five years, he has commuted over an hour each way for ten- to twelve-hour days on the shop floor. Justin and I led manufacturing for a year when we first started, but Donnie is the guy I passed the baton to, and we've never looked back.

Keeping a mobile health program running is a long way from the adrenaline rush of a real pit stop in a NASCAR race, but talk to him and you'll quickly learn he loves it.

"I tell the young guys who work here all the time about how good they have it," Wingo said. "I've worked in a lot of places with a lot of pressure and had a lot of fun. But this place is special. The people you work with every day—the nurses who are driving all over the place—they're special people."

I watched him just after he'd gotten off a Zoom call with a client, talking a young woman through how to do some maintenance work on one of the vehicles. He walked her through the operation in a way that made her feel much more confident about being on the road. I've heard of him giving up nights and weekends to help clients, taking calls at one in the morning from the West Coast. He doesn't do it for money; he does it because he is a servant leader, and servant leaders add value to others who serve.

Consider this reality for a moment—here's a man who spent more than four decades participating in literally the fastest-paced sport in the world. There is nothing more demanding than auto racing when it comes to that level of competition. Pit stops are measured in tenths of a second. Races can be won or lost by the smallest of mistakes. It is intense and exhausting. The thrill of victory has got to be mind-blowing. Yet here Wingo thrives, joyfully smiling as he instructs yet another nurse on how to check the oil in a generator. The love he has for others beams through.

That's why we hire as many NASCAR pit crew members as we can. Like Mitch Williams, who came to us after thirty years at The Legendary Garage. "You know, this is important stuff we're working on," Williams said. "And whatever a client needs, we are going to get it done. That's just how we are."

As much as Williams loves racing, there is this overwhelming sense of purpose to how he describes this work. "The vision is really clear—there are millions of Americans who don't have healthcare, and we're helping fix that. The people around here are very focused on that. I tell the guys, 'You're not going to find better work than this.' There's really a shared sense of belonging that builds up from the transparency, the trust, and how we treat each other. We're teammates."

The transparency Williams is talking about is open-book management—Amanda and I feel very strongly that we owe our team information about their job security and the impact their work has on the team that some other business owners might not share openly.

Back to Jan Rock: She was supposed to stay with us for a few weeks while getting settled in North Carolina. Five years later, she's our chief people officer, and honestly, I can't imagine the company without her. Jan didn't know anything about healthcare when she started cold-calling governors' offices. But she loves people, and she understood the mission. Watch her in action today—coordinating hiring across forty-two states, building systems that keep our team connected, ensuring every person who joins us knows they're valued—and you'll see what happens when someone discovers they're capable of far more than they ever imagined.

Neil Rotroff, our VP of marketing, came to us as an industrial designer, but what he brought was curiosity and the willingness to learn whatever it took. Today, he's helping healthcare systems understand how mobile health combined with patient-focused messaging can transform their communities.

Brad Watson, our chief revenue officer, exemplifies this growth. When Brad joined us, he was, as he says, "good with people." But unlike others who simply sold equipment, he chose to immerse himself in understanding the human challenges our clients face. Now when he talks to health system CEOs, he's partnering with them to help solve problems no amount of check-writing could ever accomplish. He's become a leader in our field, and with our team, because he was willing to grow beyond his comfort zone.

Justin Schultz, our VP of engineering, started as an engineer, with a decade of specialty vehicle experience under his belt. But Justin is bigger on the inside than he had ever been allowed to be on the outside. He immediately started asking questions about workflow optimization, equipment integration, and how the physical design of a mobile health clinic might improve patient experience. Today he's not just an engineer—he's a healthcare innovator.

Aaron Reed, our director of innovation, took that same approach. He saw that innovation was less about better equipment and more about better systems, better processes, and educating people.

The pattern became clear: Give people a mission bigger than themselves, invest in their growth, and watch them grow as leaders in ways they never expected. That's how we ended up with people like Maria Ferraris as executive director of our research consortium. Maria doesn't just coordinate mobile health research studies; she is a thought leader, helping establish an evidence base for mobile health that didn't exist twelve months ago.

Brad Anderson, executive director of our Global Mobile Healthcare Association and leader of our Project Echo program, didn't simply create an association—he created a platform where practitioners could connect and learn. Mollie Williams, executive director of Mobile Health Map, didn't just build a database—she built a foundation for evidence-based mobile health research that is on its way to tremendous heights.

Troy Watson, our director of field operations, spent a first career in the US Army and a second in law enforcement. He's a strong believer in public service and the work we're doing. When Joshua Chancey, our senior director of contracts and a former Army Ranger, is working with a health system on a complex financing arrangement, he's not just negotiating terms—he's building relationships, understanding their challenges, and finding ways to add value beyond the contract. Bruce Harbin, our senior director of engineering, doesn't just manage engineering projects—he understands how his work impacts our financial performance, our client relationships, and our mission. Bruce Berger, our director of manufacturing, sees how quality control in manufacturing affects customer satisfaction scores, which affects revenue growth, which affects our ability to hire more people and expand our mission.

And Rett, and Lynn, and Monica, and Mykayla, and Jacki. And Ben. And Ruben. And Mike. And Dario. And Wendy. And Alvin. And Cowboy. And Eduardo. You get the picture.

The healthcare industry veterans who joined us brought something different but equally valuable. Brian Toomey, the retired CEO of Piedmont Health, could have spent his retirement golfing. Instead, he sees the potential of mobile health and wants to help our clients avoid mistakes he made in the past. Dr. Paul McGann, retired chief medical officer from CMS's Center for Quality Innovation, didn't just lend us credibility—he helped us understand how to navigate the complex world of healthcare policy and payment. Adam Barefoot, our chief dental officer (former CDO at HRSA and the

Georgia State Department of Public Health) adds tremendous value and depth to the work.

And Matt Bailey, our unofficial "Chairman of the Board," has always helped me see the field and evaluate our opportunities with clear eyes.

These are people who caught a vision of what was possible. Every single person I've mentioned started somewhere else and is now on their way to becoming something more. That's not an accident. That's the result of a very intentional approach to valuing people and investing in their growth.

Now here's the surprise I promised you at the beginning.

Our vision is "to deliver healthcare to every American in every corner of our country." That's what we're working toward, what we're building toward.

But our mission—our daily purpose, our reason for existing—is something completely different. Our mission is to "build the world's greatest place to work."

That might sound backward to you. You'd think a healthcare company's mission would be about healthcare. But many times, success is counterintuitive. "Always invert," as Berkshire Hathaway legend Charlie Munger would say.[67]

If we want to change healthcare, we must find people who believe what we believe—shared values—that we are people of value who value all people.

First, we must **appreciate them for who they are**—not just for what they can do for us but for their inherent worth as human beings.

67 Charles T. Munger, *Poor Charlie's Almanack: The Wit and Wisdom of Charles T. Munger*, ed. Peter D. Kaufman, expanded 3rd ed. (Walsworth, 2005).

Second, we must **believe that they will do their very best**—we must believe in them and have faith in their potential before they believe in themselves.

Third, we must **care about them as individuals**—know their families, their dreams, their challenges.

Fourth, we must **develop them intentionally** because growth doesn't just happen—it must be planned and purposeful. Rarely does anyone succeed by accident.

And fifth, we must **equip them for success**—give them the tools, training, and opportunities they need to thrive. Put great leaders in front of them as examples.

This is what John Maxwell advocates in his book *High Road Leadership*—the idea that true leaders value people above their own agenda, wanting more for the people they serve than they expect in return. Put people above your own agenda and prioritize their well-being and growth. That's servant leadership.

Some will stay with us and continue growing our vision. Others will leave and start their own companies, join other organizations, or launch initiatives we never could have imagined. Either way, the impact multiplies.

That's our formula for building a workplace where (1) you recognize $125 million in revenue in forty-two states in less than five years and (2) your stomach doesn't hurt on Sunday night.

This is a group of winners. If you're in this space, you want people like these on your team to help you help the ones you care about most.

You don't change the world by doing everything yourself but by bringing others around you who share the belief that, together, you can accomplish things beyond your wildest dreams.

We'll see you out there.

Acknowledgments

To Jan Rock—you answered the phone in the middle of a pandemic and never stopped showing us how much you love us. You moved across the country and became Mission Mobile teammate number one. You didn't just believe in us. You showed up and played hard every day. We love you.

To Neil Rotroff—the day I was fired, you walked into my office and said, "That's not cool. Where are we going?" For a guy with very few friends, that means everything. We love you and your family.

To Brad and Lindsay Watson—you joined us early when it was super risky. Brad, you've taken every tough assignment, taken us to market, and never once made me doubt your values, character, or integrity. Partners like you are rare. We love you and your family.

To John Maxwell—you've been my mentor for over a decade. Your fingerprints are all over this company, this book, and my soul. When you taught me serving others was the highest calling, you changed how I lived and led. Everything worthwhile in these pages traces back to what you've poured into me. But as I've heard you say, "No royalties, though!" We love you and Margaret.

To Don Yaeger and Jason Cole—you helped us find the story inside the story. Your craft made this book what it is. We couldn't have written this book and told these stories without you.

To the healthcare leaders who trusted us with their stories—Dr. Nancy Oriol, Dr. Coley King, David Vliet, Dr. Levy, Jerry Isikoff, Dr. Jamie-Colina, and the entire Family Van team. You blazed the trail. We're just trying to smooth the path. We love you.

To the Mission Mobile team—you look forward to Monday mornings. That's not normal, and it's not an accident. You're changing the world. We love you and your families.

To everyone who serves the underserved—the community health workers, nurses, physician assistants, and doctors who get up every day to take care of people who need you most. This book is for you. We love you. You're not alone.

About the Authors

Travis and Amanda LeFever are the founders of Mission Mobile Medical Group, a healthcare infrastructure company that grew from startup to $100 million in revenue in less than five years.

Their journey began unexpectedly. After Travis's father died of a heart attack at only sixty-six in a rural community with limited healthcare access, Travis resolved to live differently. When he was fired from his turnaround role at a specialty vehicles company, he and Amanda incorporated a mobile healthcare company the first week of March 2020. The next week, the country shut down for COVID-19.

What followed was a five-year immersion into why healthcare works for some Americans and fails so many others. The LeFevers have worked alongside street medicine providers, health system executives, federal policymakers, and the frontline clinicians who show up every day to serve some of our most vulnerable neighbors who live in hard-to-reach places.

Mission Mobile Medical Group now holds an ARPA-H contract as System Integrator for PARADIGM program—the largest federal mobile health innovation program in history. Travis and Amanda operate the company from North Carolina, where they live with their brilliant, bold, beautiful, and hardworking daughter London.

They believe the mobile health model can help America rediscover the benefits of servant leadership.

For Further Reference

Bondjers, K., Ingebjørg Lingaas, Synne Stensland, et al. "'I've kept going' – A Multisite Repeated Cross-Sectional Study of Healthcare Workers' Pride in Personal Performance During the COVID-19 Pandemic." *BMC Health Services Research* 23, no. 322 (2023). https://bmchealthservres.biomedcentral.com/articles/10.1186/s12913-023-09246-5.

Centers for Medicare & Medicaid Services. "Medicare Shared Savings Program Continues to Deliver Meaningful Savings and High-Quality Health Care." Press release. October 29, 2024. https://www.cms.gov/newsroom/press-releases/medicare-shared-savings-program-continues-deliver-meaningful-savings-and-high-quality-health-care.

CMS Financial Report - Fiscal Year 2024 (Centers for Medicare & Medicaid Services, 2024). https://www.cms.gov/files/document/cms-financial-report-fiscal-year-2024.pdf.

Digital Empowerment and Inclusion Working Group Broadband Access Report (Federal Communications Commission, 2023). https://www.fcc.gov/sites/default/files/cedc-digital-empowerment-inclusion-wg-broadband-access-report-06152023.pdf.

FCC Fact Sheet, *Inquiry Concerning Deployment of Advanced Telecommunications Capability to All Americans in a Reasonable and Timely Fashion.* 2024 Section 706 Report, GN Docket No. 22-270 (Federal Communications Commission, 2024). https://docs.fcc.gov/public/attachments/DOC-400675A1.pdf.

Federal Communications Commission. "Bridging the Digital Divide." https://www.fcc.gov/about-fcc/fcc-initiatives/homework-gap-and-connectivity-divide.

Higgins, Abigail, Middy Tilghman, and Tracy Kuo Lin. "Mobile Health Clinics in a Rural Setting: A Cost Analysis and Time Motion Study of La Clinica in Oregon, United States." *BMC Health Services Research* 25, no. 1 (2025): 97. https://bmchealthservres.biomedcentral.com/articles/10.1186/s12913-024-12203-5.

Lee, Jun Soo, Ami Bhatt, Lisa M. Pollack, et al. "Telehealth Use During the Early COVID-19 Public Health Emergency and Subsequent Health Care Costs and Utilization." *Health Affairs Scholar* 2, no. 1 (2024). https://academic.oup.com/healthaffairsscholar/article/2/1/qxae001/7560333.

Parth, M. N. "Doctors' new tool to treat homeless people: A medical clinic in a van." *LA Times*, July 25, 2022.

Song, Zirui, Caterina Hill, Jennifer Bennet, Anthony Vavasis, and Nancy E. Oriol. "Mobile Clinic in Massachusetts Associated with Cost Savings from Lowering Blood Pressure and Emergency Department Use." *Health Affairs* 32, no. 1 (2013): 36–44. https://www.healthaffairs.org/doi/abs/10.1377/hlthaff.2011.1392.

Venice Family Clinic. "VFC Street Medicine." https://venicefamilyclinic.org/street-medicine/ https://venicefamilyclinic.org/street-medicine/.

Unless otherwise indicated, all interviews and quotations contained herein were conducted exclusively for the purposes of this book and have been included with the knowledge and consent of those quoted.

www.ingramcontent.com/pod-product-compliance
Lightning Source LLC
LaVergne TN
LVHW090604110826
845146LV00001B/260

9798891886216